Nubian Americans Identity Rise

Albert Fortney Jr.

Scripture quotations marked KJV are from the Holy Bible, King James Version (Authorized Version). First published in 1611. Quoted from the KJV Classic Reference Bible, Copyright © 1983 by The Zondervan Corporation.

Any people depicted in stock imagery provided by Thinkstock are models, and such images are being used for illustrative purposes only. Certain stock imagery © Thinkstock.

Orders can be placed via email: Orders@Albertfortneyjr.com or www.albertfortneyjr.com. Also available on Amazon. The Fortney Encyclical History Ed. Co. expresses its great pride in research.

CONTENTS

**He ain't heavy
He's my brother**

He ain't heavy,
He's my
brother

Africa under full glacial conditions

Africa under full glacial conditions was North Africa before the White man dug-out the Suez Canal that wrongly dismantled geographically part of the African Continent, Africa rejected too. Because 250 miles offshore is larger than France; Island Madagascar still is the African Continent.

Egypt Sinai Peninsula

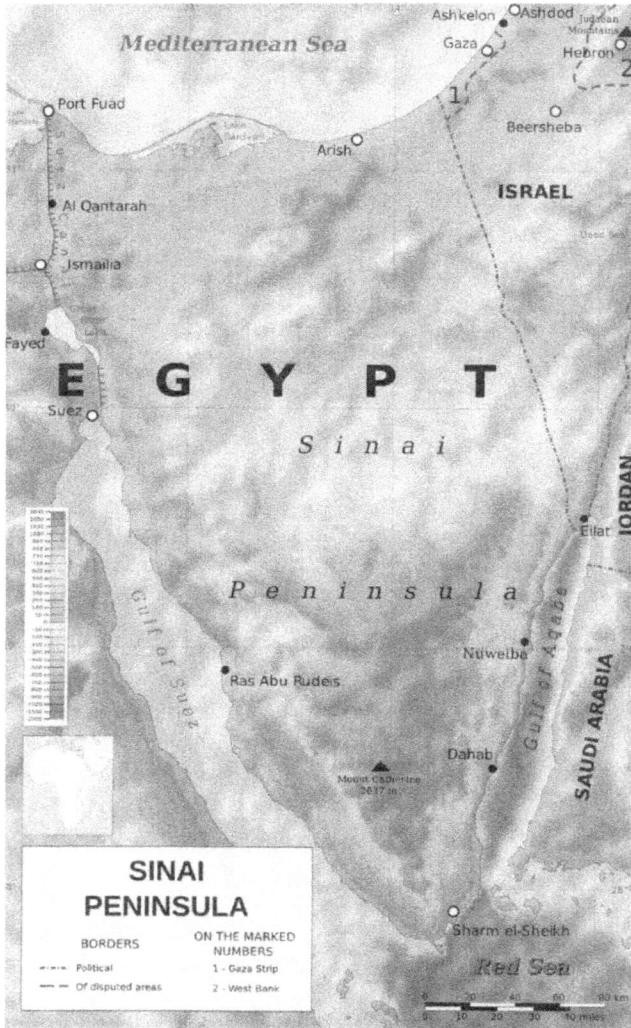

Mediterranean Sea

Ashkelon Ashdod Judean Mountains
Gaza Hebron
2
1
Port Fuad
Beersheba
Arish
ISRAEL
Al Qantarah
Dead Sea
Ismailia
Fayed
E G Y P T
Suez
S i n a i
JORDAN
Eilat
P e n i n s u l a
Gulf of Suez
Gulf of Aqaba
Nuweiba
Ras Abu Rudeis
SAUDI ARABIA
Dahab
Mount Catherine
2637 m
Sharm el-Sheikh
Red Sea

SINAI
PENINSULA

BORDERS	ON THE MARKED NUMBERS
Political	1 - Gaza Strip
Of disputed areas	2 - West Bank

INTRODUCTION – The Fortney Encyclical History Ed. Co.

The Black Man's historian concern of his world history, demands the attention to his **kinky wooly-hair image** as the **"Nubian American identity."** Means a recognition **not** here, as <u>African</u> <u>Americans</u>. **No longer** the use of African American a **continent's** <u>title</u>; of a descriptive but not an **"identity"** usage for the importance in education, resource power, prehistory & ancient great achievements till today; and especially black businesses in America, with a **mark of distinction** that stands for **"NUBIAN."** Threw-out U.S. history, Nubian Americans have **blessed** America.

Cush (Kush), is the name of a once great ancient kingdom in **"Northeast Africa."** According to the Bible, Cush was the son of Ham a descendant to her neighbor, Ethiopia. By the Greeks, "Cushi" is a **HEBREW** term for a black person. As late as the 1940s and 50s, the racial identity of Nubians were and remained problematic for "white" scholars; even when bones of Kushite royalty were recovered from the "Reisner's excavations" and sent to specialists at the Museum of Harvard, they identified them as belonging to the "basic white stock of Egypt." White scholars left no doubt about their biases to dismiss the Nubian rule of Egypt's 25th Dynasty "black kings;" now recognized as the renaissance of Egyptian's great engineering, art, and culture. They soon figured-out how to appease wooly-haired black's resentment of being called colored, blacks and Negroes with a pacifying permissible, incorrect usage of African Americans.

Know this absolute wisdom, that the Nubian American of the African Continents past Biblical Cush Empire, is the unseen space "Alien" by the white man's History Channel, who's creative blackness is overlooked and seems unrecognizable to the 6,000 years old bias Caucasian. That there must be something else as smart as white but certainly not black; even though all the facts points to the contrary!!! Just like, not up-dating "schoolroom text," that the Egyptian Nubian great pyramid was a "nuclear power-plant," and not a royal burial ground. Was unrecognizable to explain without recent modern-day knowledge of nuclear "isotopes." The high intelligence, of prehistory black man scientists also created the blonde-hair blue eyed Aryan in 600 years on Patmos Island; with "graftation" of blacks to white that Islam in detail explains, what National Geographic's verified his first appearance 6,000 yrs. ago; he **omits** in his story of history. He'd rather depict from an **ape**, while whitewashing black <u>lands and history</u> as his…he can't about us <u>Nubians</u>. This time wherever the truth was lost, here's the **WHOLE** truth.

If they don't feel guilty or have no remorse over the <u>evil</u> they've done and **"lying"** on us then we, don't feel guilty on telling the truth about their **'birth'** and <u>evil</u> <u>deeds</u> that follow almost all of them. **White nationalism racists** are trying to <u>steal</u> "democracy of freedom" away from black and brown people, for the white privileged and **white supremacist**. Jan. 6, 2021 was a **death** day **'insurrection'** of the capital building, by **racist American terrorists**. Their objective is removal of the vote and blocking black and people of color from obtaining "resource power" under a <u>guise</u> of Christian conservative's supporting a **fascist** like leader **Trump** (Ashkenazi Jew), claiming it's justifiable for a <u>pure</u> "white America." You play by good rules, law and deed to move forward.

.

The Fortney Encyclical History Ed. Co.

"America's Best Kept Secret – Nubian Americans." History has not been recorded fairly of the wooly-hair black-man, but kind only for the white-man because "they" have written it in many instances a fiction (lie) they settled upon in agreeing. For 500 years, they have <u>insultingly</u> <u>manipulated</u> their image, story, and texts of so-called history to the majority population; black and brown people of the world. St. John 8: 44 – Ye are of *your* father the devil, and the lusts of your father ye will do. …a murderer… there is no truth in him…he is a liar and the father of it.

We're describing Euro-Caucasians and Semite white looking southwestern Asian Jew nomad converts to Judaism of the Black Hebrew religion. Rev. 2: 9 – I know thy works, and tribulation, and poverty, (but thou art rich) and *I know* the blasphemy of them…say they are Jews, and are not, but *are* the synagogue of Satan. Once ancient biblical Cush (Kush), is now called SUDAN; the largest country in Africa. Nubia (Sudan), is what the ancient Romans called it and in Africa.

In 1909, American Euro-Egyptologist George Reisner said that, Nubia was governed by "white" Libyans in Africa, mind you who supposedly created this black ancient civilization. Then later changed to a black governed people. The place where hieroglyphic writing was first discovered, where magnificent temples and mastery of pyramids were already built while Egypt was in its infancy didn't know existed as the original "cradle of the arts, sciences, and civilization," is kept from being depicted as **"black-skin"** text in the American school systems.

The devious of evil in Caucasian and Semite rule, created its made-up, false "cradle of civilization" area around the Tigris and Euphrates Rivers (once was **Africa**), in Iraq, 3,000 B.C.

Mesopotamia. By-passed by omitting, the 5,000 B.C. Nubian established civilization, of a true **"wooly-hair"** black-man history. Why, is the rich history of Nubia overlooked for **"Nubian Americans"** rightful identity; wrongly called African American (as a "lost identity")?

Great black "Nubian Queens" were, Shanakdakhete, Tiye, Amani Rina, and Kandake Amanirenas, who skillfully defended her kingdom against "Caesar's Roman Empire" from conquering her homeland. And several wooly-hair "Nubian Kings" ruled Egypt's 25th Dynasty.

The new hydroelectric Kajabar Dam, located 250 miles south of the Egyptian-Sudanese border in Sudan, will cover with water dozens of their last remaining villages and inhumane, brazenly displacing tens of thousands of people, Nubians "protest." The Kajabar Dam will also flood ancient Nubian monuments, along with other antiquities dating to 5,000 years ago. "There are no Nubians in the dam area. There are only Arabic tribes. "Lied," they are not the original Nubians," says (paid) Al-Khatim Abdullah press adviser to Sudanese Embassy in Cairo, Egypt.

The government has not provided a relocation project, he says, because it still needs funding. However, risks to the great Nubian culture remain. Think about this enough to respond because Nubians will need all the help they can get. Rightly and adequately preserve, their outstanding first in creative traditions. The grand historian author, February 18, 2022 (Friday).

****

The Fortney Encyclical History Ed. Co. – "Theme Topic"

"America's next best kept secret – Nubian American's identity." **Identity Means Everything.** It's Northeast Africa's Nubia (Sudan's biblical Cush [Kush]), of ancient 5,000 BC – 500 AD geography of history to visit. Is a fact, the most important to view of ancient "wooly-haired black skin history," that represents the greatest people of today, is the "Nubian American."

Anti-black racists deem anything in an ancient black-man culture, or African black context is in their view doesn't have the meaning, it obviously have, to them is other than Africa. Nubians (Cushites), were excellent bow and arrow archers of war and were characterized largely as a militaristic people in the Hebrew Bible. Military engagement references to Cush (2 Chronicles 14:9-15; Isaiah 20:3-4; Jeremiah 46:9; Ezekiel 30:4-5, 38:5; Nahum 3:9). Isaiah 18:2 characterizes the Cushite people was **"feared near and far,"** and a mighty nation of conquering, **"supreme."**

Joel 2:25 God promises that He will restore all that was taken away in the years that the devil was tearing down the "church." Biblical Ethiopia (Nubia) is Genesis 10. God is reforming to bring restoration of the original faith and away from European "tradition" and "theology."

Nubian military reputation was consistent in ancient Egypt and had spread throughout the ancient Near East. However, far from skin-color hate we see in the physical characteristics racist concerns today, the Ancient Cushite (Nubian), Egyptians, Assyrians, and Greeks had NO negative racist black nor white skin-color racialized view of identity. **Identity Knows History!!!**

Amos 9:7, presents an almost sameness between black wooly-hair Israelites and Cushites: Are you not like the Cushites to me, O Israel, declares our Lord, Yahweh, Christ. But Rabbinate (Ashkenazi of Genesis 10:3) provides their explanation: "Israel's Christ is no more than his own uncivilized, and despised black race of Ethiopians"...and the fact that wooly-hair "slaves" were so often made of them added to despising them. In the 15th century AD, Gentiles created <u>racism</u>.

Also the beliefs of today's modern influence, and unwarranted assumptions always remind us, are the ancient Cushites until today's wooly-hair <u>Nubian</u> Americans, once "despised" black <u>slaves</u>. This trajectory was from biblical observation into the 20th century till today, explicit anti-black racist sentiments are directly to Nubian Americans (ex-Negros, ex-African Americans).

Ancient Nubian identity by black and brown people, was also by their wooly afro-textured kinky <u>hair</u>. Cornrow and braided hairstyles, were historically worn to signify marital status, age, religion, wealth and rank was an important sacred spiritual symbol that was proudly worn.

In Amos 9:7, Israel is compared in sameness to Cush because both nations will experience Yahweh's (Jesus Christ) judgment and salvation. The Amos passage teaches us that ancient identities are specified ethnically, nationally, tribal, in **stone** or geographically because it is too convenient for interpreters to put or read "their own values" into biblical text. A man, is supposed to be the symbol of <u>strength</u>, **truth.** The Nubian American (descendant of Cushites), is said more, **"<u>righteous</u> <u>by</u> <u>nature</u>."**

****

The Fortney Encyclical History Ed. Co. - Research

Our company represents, **"We the People,"** seekers of truth. Truth are Nubian American's experiences for the best interest, and their light for the world that will set you free; is like food with the bodies mechanism, that creates energy for the body to function and perform. **"The Truth Is The Light."** Anything else is a so-called, <u>alternate</u>-<u>truth</u> (fiction, a lie, untrue, incorrect, false and just plain wrong). This so-called truth (lies), is why black people are despised and hated to death by racist and white nationalist changing of black history as they choose…

Asks the question, why are all King James Version biblical characters depicted Caucasians? Another thing, America is teaching its children an <u>alternate</u>-<u>truth</u> in education that supposedly is properly teaching students, how to think correctly and grow, to function and perform in life. They have actually applied this <u>alternate</u>-<u>truth</u> in "history."

Whether they realize it or not, they're subconsciously and indirectly teaching <u>hate</u> to <u>despise</u> black people; by leaving out the black man's great cultural accomplishments in Africa's past and first civilization; instead of constant expounding on <u>servitude</u> and demeaning **<u>slavery;</u>** that they believe is good enough and deserving of black people. Black lives does matter and those against it, must stand accountable for their guilt, of their backwards evil actions and atrocities.

The atrocities we deem responsible against black people's progression also are:

1. Unseen targeting of domestic sanctions by crippling business resources that causes unemployment
2. Manipulate unjust and unbalanced law and order equality against black and brown peoples

3. Restrict black man's cultural "knowledge of self," with abuse of power depicting religion with a white-supremacy "misleading history narrative," in educational institutions and entertainment medias
4. Institute a much poorer-black educational system, to hinder, the invaluable role to children's education make
5. Implement poisonous health conditions, by living in locations of placement, close to industrial toxins

All these sufferings are preventable by the constitution. Black and brown people can't stand for none of this and must echo loud our thoughts. It's said amongst all black people, that we have to be "twice as good to get ahead;" to make-up for obstacles whites will put in your way they couldn't do, if the other way around. However, we are succeeding, but not fast enough with systemic racist roadblocks. America must stop, rationalizing away its responsibility to take action for we the people starts now, immediately today, and not the "stuff-off" with soon or tomorrow. We don't have to love but we must **"respect each other"** in order to **co-exist** should be a common understanding but taught **"a priority"** with the first amendment protecting freedom of speech.

A sixth grade student in Florida told a substitute teacher he wouldn't stand for the pledge because he believed the American flag symbolized discrimination against blacks. He was arrested because he started a disturbance police claimed. Atheistic or religious freedom groups tried to eliminate the phrase "under God" from the pledge. The first amendment shouldn't protect blasphemous and fraudulent depicted text, of black-man's original cultural heritage history as a fictional (lie) white-man's creation that does extreme harm to the "original belief." If so, would it not represent **"double-jeopardy,"** to permit a <u>white-supremacy</u>-<u>exception</u> to the rules of the first amendment rights; to rewrite with pictured deceptive white history as his own, of black history???

Racism was created in Europe during the 15ᵗʰ century Middle Ages to deceive, that gave way to doing harm, hurt and despising of Africa's black man, especially it's Sudan (Nubia) ancient Cush history (Nubian American ex-Negro) world-wide. It seems, English biblical scholars (King James Version) try to keep Cushites other than a reference to Mesopotamia and only to identify to lands south of Egypt. It was their planning to wrongly justify a so-called "garden of Eden" all theirs "cradle of civilization in Mesopotamia" opposed to the true cradle of civilization south of Egypt in Nubia (Ethiopia), and an Israel Semite now, was once a **wooly-hair** ancient Nubian land. Parts of **Arabia** was once a part or region of **Africa,** and most certainly **Israel** (major land of Levant) was before the white-man carved-out the Suez Canal and deviously claimed (with poor excuses) it separated, Israel from the great black-man's **"Africa Continent."**

In early ancient times, skin-color wasn't a relevant issue or factor in identifying a people was rare, like in the life time of Christ the wooly-hair, black-skin color liberator. (Rev. 1:14-15 KJV) His head and *his* hairs *were* white like wool, as white as snow; and his eyes *were* as a flame of fire; 15 And his feet like unto fine brass, as if they burned in a furnace; and his voice as the sound of many waters.

Skin color back then was like hair color today, of seeing it but not really mentioning it. However, there really are no white people in the Holy Bible. Abraham, Moses, King Solomon, Deborah, Sheba, David, Elijah, Jezebel, Daniel, Jesus, Peter, Paul or Lydia and even the church **Rome** were not white; because whiteness hadn't existed yet, was thought of as **"tribes"** or **"nations"** Greek for nation is "ethnos" (ethnic). Some historical roots were cultural overlaps. Racism, was a baseless theory of putting white people at the top of the scale, red and yellow in between and black people at the very bottom.

Historically, white U.S.A. historian text teaches that their keen, they think, to up-play physical characteristics with Caucasian figures in the Bible, to manifest superiority of white spirituality. **"<u>Satan</u>,"** however being the prince of darkness is represented as a horned, winged black-man like figure to <u>despise</u> and <u>hate</u> is a white-man's <u>manufactured</u> image. To see a <u>devil</u> and his followers in life like movies would seem terrifying for an audience but an exhilarating experience for white nationalist, KKK terrorists or white supremacy racists.

The History Channel's **"<u>The</u> <u>Bible</u>"** mini-series did just that, with Moroccan actor Mohamen Medi Ouazanni (convenient to mar with envy, a President Obama look-alike), played the part of **Satan**. Dr. Martin Luther King Jr., emphasized that the color of one's skin doesn't determine the content of one's character. His statement attacked, the language and negative image of Nubian Americans men, women, and children that associated them to "<u>darkness with demonic evil</u>," and "whiteness with good." Across medieval Europe, they described <u>Satan</u> as dark or black.

The "<u>dark</u> <u>arts</u>," were known of <u>witches</u> in early colonial America. <u>Satan</u> did not only come in blackness or a red-devil, he could take any number of forms he needed. This had to have paved the way collectively for Caucasian and Semite children to grow up subconsciously if not direct <u>attitudes</u> with <u>hate</u> for the black-man; but gives no-excuse as he learned or instinctively knew, from his fabricated history that, he knows better than that!!!

<u>Racist</u> sufferings are preventable. We the people must not stand

for none of this with action. We must echo loud our thoughts or indifference may to some other than black or brown, you're **"next."** War is <u>Satan</u>, **God help Ukraine...**

"To My Nubian Queen"

To a most *deserving lady* perhaps one day her speech, through a microphone on stage that represents *"perseverance"* makes you *"__rightfully known__,"* might go a little something like this:

The *"Fortney Encyclical History Ed. Co."* drums bellows their beat, loud across the U.S., with our deep concern to **"__educate__."** But keeping humility in mind with the **facts,** of major events and achievements. Many times hidden and standing in the back of the line from history; such as the "distinct wooly-hair trait" of **Nubian American's** (so-called ex-negroes). The **Sudan's** great and glorious ancient history still stands, also a great part of us being here is, **we the people.**

Just as if yes, there's a "__secret__ __cold__-__war__" going on against us who are striving to only do good and not informed is a deadly wrong. Has the markings of old evil __Satan__ and his diligent servant __devils__, against us same old but "more-righteous" **"wooly-hair"** people created in "God's image."

There is too much unnecessary things going-on that lack a common-decency, respect, and empathy towards those of color with __evil__ __racism__. Being **Caucasian** or **Semite-Jew,** you wouldn't put on yourself. You have shown an increase in discrimination even during humanitarian crisis globally. You cry of "democracy," yet you are not the one swimming in those same dangerously turmoil waters, nor are you racked across hot coals of __whitewashed__ __racism.__ Is your __hypocrisy,__ you continuously subject us Nubian American's… Forgiveness is costly and never is it forgotten.

Our prestigious history books for adults and the children's

book of black history is astounding. Our books the Fortney Encyclical History Ed. Co. carry, are shining examples almost (so to speak) bursting at their seams with enlightenment, deserving to all people of different nationalities to service, **we the people!** Don't hesitate, "learn the sacred truth from **slavery** **to** **racism** of all time we are living in." And we also have concern for the <u>sad</u> people incarcerated, society has written off, are all God's children in His sight, in dire need of our book's learning that will help them.

Nubian American's, the **Nubian,** is a Godly people's history. The hair like lamb's wool Nubian civilization flourished in **Sudan** over 5,000 years ago **Africa,** was well before the birth of **Egypt.** The time spam may be off at least 10 to 12,000 years old, instead of the great pyramid's age being 2500 to 3000 years old by mainstream scientist's inaccuracy. It's known, the great pyramid and the Sphinx were built by them before the great flood, during the ice-age about 12,000 years ago. Nubians were great warriors and rulers of Egypt's 25th Dynasty. The "Turin Papyrus Map" is one of the oldest (1,600 BC) maps known, is of a "gold" mine in Nubia. Then why was Africa's great Nubian civilization completely bye-passed in American taught schoolhouse learning??

The white man's world history is a whitewashed (lie), favored to others (Semite-Jews) about us (Nubians), well before him the Caucasian was created 6,600 years ago, in small comparison. Africa's **pre-history** of black-skin Egyptians were original Nubian descendants, and not today's light-skin ad-mixtures of southwestern Asians, Semite Arabs, or Semite Euro-Jews <u>despising</u> us. Nubians, **creators** of engineering, math, law, the sciences, and religion before Egypt's honorable mentions, after us inspiring Nubians.

What is the real reason or why am I so <u>despised</u> and so <u>hated</u> like so-called jungle <u>savages</u>; as to keep <u>hidden</u> and <u>steal</u> my "true identity" locked away with my "great cultural heritage" from me in <u>slavery</u>; as being a **"Nubian American,"** and not colored or Negro and always only the "N" word nigger (at a black lynching) to <u>racist</u> whites, anything but Nubian American's "rightfully so?" Because the world's foremost astonishing great collection, of Nubian antiquities are at the **Boston Museum of Fine Arts (MFA)** in the 1980's however, bias projections led to racist convictions that considered Sub-Saharan Sudan's Nubia of Africa, a barbarized shadow of Egypt by European virtue of too much "Negro" infusion.

White America wants to accentuate Eurocentric reality even when it comes to all white biblical characters you view in a pictorial bible, makes no sense to truth, which represents a racist view towards ancient black kingdoms, cultures and nations till today must end. A rarity, but some wooly-hair Nubians have blue around the pupil of their eyes. And some of his Ethiopian ancestry neighbor's hair, is straight are facts of black Africa's genetics not explained in mainstream science.

What is white <u>racism</u> against a dark white? Here's a brief view, of a confusing understanding of "whites" <u>racism</u>, besides <u>anti</u>-Semite and <u>anti</u>-Nubian Americans. During the mid-19th to mid-20th century, race scientists and most anthropologists classified the European people and their descendants, "light whites" of Northern Europe with the "dark white" of the Mediterranean **"Slaves"** (the first slaves of history), were referred to as subhuman, and Eastern European countries such as Poland, Ukraine and the USSR (Russian) etc. was do, to the racial inferiority of their inhabitants was, to evil-rule doings.

Germany and Fascist **Italy** both had the same view, to falsely justify their colonial ambitions in Eastern Europe on racist anti-Slavic grounds were also not alone in this view. **<u>Racism</u>**, is the rawest and worst of devious evils to all races of peoples of the world that was prophesized and recorded by biblical historian scholars of ancient Sudan Cushite (**Nubians**). The Nazi, categorized the world's black and brown human races as "<u>not human</u>" and so <u>evil</u> (the Euro-Jews) as to deserve <u>extermination</u>; World War II's extreme of <u>racism's</u> **genocide,** goes against **"God's Law."**

Everyone should know, that humans did NOT <u>evolve</u> from animals and animals have "fur" not **"hair,"** and if you remove the fur from monkey or ape (the unbelievable Darwin theory) their skin is pale white; so where does that leave the black man, certainly not coming from the white man. Clearly then, the wooly like, knotty (chiseled balls of hair knots for beards & hair in stone), or kinky hair is his **"proof"** that's so important. The **Nubians** were the "original humans" (made in **God's image** and known, more "righteous in nature" and with empathy) that asks the question (another issue) who was talking to whom when in the bible it said, **"Let us make man?"**

Nubian is able to create black, brown, red, yellow and white. While a white man and another Caucasian creates only Caucasian, is a fact of uncontestable truth. Whether there was a **natural selection** in migration of tribes that became different skin-colors, by black and brown progression of genetic mating or either the **grafting** theory of **Yakub;** who brought about the white race is now accepted his first appearance anywhere was 6,600 years ago.

The word Caucasian is actually a 19th century anthropological idea. It was based around a <u>false</u> conception that the origin of the human species was in the **Caucasus Mountains…** "Caucasians" is a <u>white</u> <u>supremacist</u>, <u>racist</u> ideology. Scientist found that the earliest humans didn't come from the Caucasus but from Sudan **Africa,** in modern day **Ethiopia** (Eden). Race is not supported by science. All peoples are of one species (Human). Humans are 99.9% identical in genetic make-up.

"Jesus Christ Acknowledged Being Nubian:" Though we already learned previously that there's so many times Ethiopia is represented and stood for the Biblical translation **Cush/Nubia,** and even the English King James version translate "Ethiopia for Cush," in Genesis 2:13. Black **"Moses"** married a **Cushite** woman (Numbers 12:1). And here is where, during the millennial rein of **Christ, Jesus** will receive honor from **Cush/Ethiopia:** "From beyond the rivers of Cush my worshipers, my scattered people, will bring me offerings" (Zephaniah 3:10). Most certainly should be a great **"Biblical Sunday School Lesson"** around the whole-wide world to children.

True history depiction for elementary and high schooling learning that "teaches students how to think," should include a curriculum of the Sub-Saharan Africa, to Egypt and the Mediterranean civilizations as **"Nubian Study."** Giving all children a "same" chance to succeed. We're the renowned **Nubian Americans** of ex-slaves; whose ancestors contributed great accomplishments, advances to civilization itself that some are **marvels** modern man mysteries today can't solve such as the architect of the great, over 12,000 yrs. old **Pyramid** and **Sphinx** of Giza, Egypt. We built America with our blood, sweat and tears. It's a history that should be recognized in all institutions of learning around the world, because anything else would be **"uncivilized."**

The Euro-white man is trying to say he's a part of Mesopotamians, who are typically by him considered the very first urban (city) civilization along with the Sumerians in the world is fiction. It is a made-up and manufactured lie to eliminate, avoid telling or to get around by causing an Africa's black man's history of "<u>confusion</u>," to how he (whites) were **created;** when in the Bible blacks saying to other blacks said, **"Let us make man."** The white man is trying to fit himself in his history, as Caucasian "creating civilization." How dumb-founded he must feel saying he came from an <u>ape</u>, when he was a **Nubian/Egyptian** creation world's first civilization.

Fossil remains say the first human was the 2 million years ago Africa's black man, who supposedly appeared as modern-day man 200,000 was in Sub-Saharan Nubia/Ethiopia; and not a Euro-manufactured "cradle of civilization" in Mesopotamia's **Levant** (Israel, Iraq, Syria or Turkey etc.) called modern-day Anatolia. Despite humans living there longer than anywhere else, the **Sub-Saharan African** built advanced civilizations are systematically <u>denied</u> and <u>downplayed</u> is because they are the <u>hidden</u> identity by whites, of the Nubian American's purposely and <u>incorrectly</u> called African Americans to try and keep a peoples great potentials <u>ignorant</u> of **"knowledge of self,"** that "<u>cripples</u>" a people's progress not knowing their strength to adequately progress, or not aware of their sense of power they possess to advance forward. **If you don't know who you are, then how the hell you know where you're going???**

Egyptians and the Great White Race Map

James Henry Breasted (1865-1935), was an American archaeologist who was regarded as one of the world's foremost authorities on the archaeology and history of Egypt and the Near East, which are collectively referred to as "the Orient." Breasted's views on the creation of Egyptian civilization by a "white race were also shared by one of his contemporaries, George Reisner. In 1916 Breasted stated Egyptians were a "brown-skinned race" and in 1935 he reversed himself and now said they were off the "Great White Race." Reisner claimed Nubia was originally governed by a dynasty of "white" Libyans, and all black dynasties were but extensions of them. Bruce Williams, an archaeological specialist of Nubian culture with the Oriental Institute decried the role racist ideologies played in distorting ancient Nile Valley history.

The Ancient Connection of Northeast Africa

This map gives the ancient connection of continental Africa to the neighboring northeastern land mass. Students, black folks and unknowing Americans have been led to believe by Western historians that Havilah (Arabia), Ethiopia, and Assyria (Mesopotamia), Persia, and Syria were separate and disconnected in their historical and geographical context, however, during biblical times they were very much connected. Since the river Niel flowed from southern Ethiopia and emptied into the Great Sea (Mediterranean) people migrated from lower Africa and journeyed to Northeast Africa (Canaan, Palestine) or today's Israel. There was no body of water to separate the two. The Suez Canal wasn't dug until the 19th century. And during War II war correspondents began to refer to North Africa and Northeast Africa as the "Middle East." The term "Middle East" disrespected by white required no need mention of Africa hence, avoid giving black recognition!

The Crucifixion

Moses the Law Giver

"Hidden Nubian Genius Rise"

The affluent ancient Nubian Empire is a vital subject of world history that was a "hidden" world history. Hidden as if forbidden beware… to always be by-passed in the schoolroom, by evil creators of "almost all untrustworthy white Christ believers." That in their evil rituals and occultism, are practiced, deceitful tactics, devious schemes and depictions of lies against truth, of the Black man; from a special continent rich in great mineral wealth, and the birth place of justice, spirituality, and intellect seems God intended an always Black man's land, "Africa."

The envies of greedy White men, are trying to claim the whole Northern part of Africa, from east to west depicted in Egyptian dress as building the great pyramid for example. The great Nubian Ethiopian blood-line Sub-Sahara, Sudan ancestor, was the world's first civilization; as God of good or the Devil with his lies know; was before either made-up Mediterrean first birth of civilization of Whites, Semite – Arab or Jew or mixing to a fiction depicted "Garden of Eden."

Then having to accept, the white skin-color assassination of the proven Black man Christ nailed and dying on the cross is parallel to like Nubian American's pain of not accepting but "forced," to view the stolen false image everywhere so much so, that the original black Christ should turn over in his grave from the insult. But is more like the double cross of Arabs to Euro-Jew owners of the slave market, had slaves delivered by Portuguese slave ship runners; causing over 100 million to their death, (over twice the population of the largest European country of Ukraine at 44 million), at the bottom of the Atlantic Ocean from abhorrent conditions aboard ship; now all the time blacks forced to seeing white police killings of unarmed, innocent black & brown men, women and children in America harms us, in the "land of the free & justice for all."

White-Jews to the contrary, hasn't suffered from racist pain since 1945 WWII, until now but why in Ukraine? Seems like some kind of balance; in a black & white "poetic justice of nature," but God bless them, in answering the question. And the dire need for Nubian American targets, must have "Victim-Laws" against police brutality "hate crimes" & "racist killings" in America.

In all of history seriousness, how's the white man going to write black man history but in all favor to himself? The answer is simple, they lied! However, the black man is rejecting the white man's perspective writing black man's history he's serving the black man, about the black man. The racist challenge emboldens us to do twice as better our job for intensely honest black man history. We have a lot to get into. We get our objective done focused on our Nubian history that must be known and getting it published for all societies to learn of their accomplishments if any. Starting from pre-history, is not hoping to be a society but is recognized, as the black essence that began in Ethiopia.

It's not as if seeming the impossible was done by blacks, but the black man did do what is thought impossible and was the first; moving unimaginable colossal carved stones with the lost genius of black technology of **"Levitation;"** is a feared feat of power, that scares the white man unable to achieve today what blacks did, so he "fantasizes a fictional lie" it must was done by some outer-space "aliens," only to discredit the Nubian's "wooly-haired genius and truth."

If anything, the alien here is the first appearance of the different white man minority on earth; and not the other way around, to the majority of people overwhelmingly with the miraculous magic performing **"Melanin,"** with a much higher count in black and brown peoples. Creates from the sun's rays into what the architect genius was, the Nubian's "gift" to his descendant neighbor, are "the great pyramids" of Giza to his Egyptian black brothers and sisters. The story of pre-history "flight" (another hidden event) and "ancient electric dry-cell batteries" discovered in "old" **Africa,** is for a later discussion. Grandmother (Bi-Ma born the month of April 1898) use to say, "Nothing is new under the sun." 'Tis true…'tis so true. He hides history, wanting us "inert" of doing our unimaginable plus, full potential to do!!!

AFFIDAVIT OF NUBIAN AMERICAN: U.S.A. Census Info.

Any question of legal argument that may arise of black-people's **"hair like lamb's wool"** confirmation of our ancestral identity as part of **we the people,** asks with all due respect recognized as **Nubian American** "identity" of a **country** (not new but to the census), and no longer as Colored, Negro or the African American "title" of a **continent** whites are also "born."

But we are a "wooly-hair" recognizable blood-line tribal **Nubian Americans**, Euro-American historians of society hide, what must change and corrected in identity schooling. They suppress from the public mass media, what even **"DNA"** technology supports. According to the Y-DNA analysis of 2008, shows that **44%** of Nubians carry haplogroup J, followed by **24%** with haplogroup E11b (also known as **E-M215**). The haplogroup J branch J-M267, is carried by Nubians is found in high ratios in North Africa, the Horn of Africa, Yemen, and Assyrians.

On the mitochondrial DNA maternal (motherly) linage **30.8** of Nubians have the **L3** mt-haplogroup, which originated in **Northeastern Africa.** Second in order, **20.6%** of Nubians have the mt-haplogroup L0a close to the "Mitochondrial Eve," significant in **South Africa, Mozambique. 10.3%** of Nubians have the **L2** clade of mt-haplogroup L, originated in **East Africa,** migrated to **West Africa,** strong in **Senegal (43-54%)**. In conclusion, they are confusingly basic **Afro-Nubian** people, having part **Niger-Congo** people and part **Bantu** people; dominate **wooly hair** – 4a to 4c ='s, exclusive to blacks of African ancestry, ex-slave **"Nubian Americans."**

They were not created yet, to tell us who we was, and so they omitted us ancient Nubians from his depicted history. We were never **conquered,** with more defining proof we wrote of us,

"chiseled in stone pre-history." There's no question of worth in the **Sudan Sub-Saharan,** to the future who's now in America; of our great **achievements,** and **ruled** Egypt in her **peak** of great history.

When most so-called African Americans take a DNA test it show they are related to ancient Nubians. Now, even DNA shows that many so-called African Americans are descendants of **"Ancient Nubians"** that out of <u>racism's</u> too many "so-called educated," miss-educated and uneducated purposely <u>ignore</u> this fact. Because no one has ever found proof of the biblical Exodus until the study of the Ancient **Cushite,** "Nubians." The Holy Bible the "Black" man wrote and Black Jewish Hebrew calls Ancient Nubia **"Goshen,"** to which is strenuously problematic for "White" groups considering themselves religiously or <u>racially</u> <u>superior</u>.

Nubian's history is well known to the white man in the western hemisphere, who's black man term we come from "Kings and Queens" represent the black man, his women and children's **"Nubian Queen"** (a flattering term) describe black people, in a <u>racist</u> hemisphere. However today, a small section of Africa's Nubians are somewhat an Arabized people but basically not a major shift since the Arab migrations into North Africa just as in Egypt.

The genetics of the Abusir el-Meleq community that did not undergo any major shifts during the **1,300-year timespan** studied, and group leader at the Max Planck Institute Krause said, "A lot of people assumed foreign invaders brought genetic ancestry into the region. People thought through time, Egypt would become more European but we see just the **exact opposite."** Modern Egyptians were found to **inherit 8%** more ancestry from **African** ancestors than the mummies studied. Increased long distanced commerce with the **Meroe** Nubian metropolis of the "gold trade" and the trans-Saharan slave trade are potential reasons why.

Half of the sub-Saharan mtDNA sequences in the database are common haplotypes that are shared among ethnic groups from multiple regions of sub-Saharan Africa. Fewer than 10% of so-called African American mtDNA matched mtDNA sequences from a single African region. Suggests that, one in nine so-called African Americans may be able to trace their mtDNA to a particular region in Africa. However, so-called African Americans mtDNA are identical to African haplotypes found in multiple ethnic groups throughout sub-Saharan Africa you can't use only mtDNA sequence information to determine a single group was the maternal ancestor.

Mitochondrial DNA tests trace people's matrilineal (mother-line) ancestry through their mitochondria, which any two people will have an identical mitochondrial DNA sequence if they are related by an unbroken maternal line. How far back can mitochondrial DNA be traced? We can trace the mtDNA back to a woman from about **150,000** to **200,000 years ago,** that everyone on the planet is related to. And the Y chromosome to a man we're all related to from **60,000** or so years ago. Scientists have named them **Mitochondrial Eve & Y Adam,** in 5/18/2012.

The percentage of human diversity between humans is about **"0.1 percent."** What we think of as "races" are socially assigned or better yet, white man sets of characteristics that change depending on context. Is race a social construct or biological? In the biological and social sciences, the consensus is very clear in history: race is a **social construct** (a white man's creation such as white supremacy racism), and not a meaningful mankind biological **attribute.**

In **anthropological** genetics, mtDNA is useful to trace

geographic distribution of genetic variation, for the investigation of expansions, migrations and other pattern of gene flow. Also, mtDNA is widely applicable in **"forensic science."** That is a powerful implement, to identify human remains that has a purposeful use that really matters.

To determine an individual's race, people may use one or more ancestry or biological bases or **physical characterizes** (most likely) and cultural bases, such as ideology and language. Race can't be found in our genes but biological ancestry is **real** that differs in race. The geographic isolation, and three great human races in the last 5,000 to 7,000 years that split our species are: **Africans** (once so-called <u>racist</u> Negroid), **Caucasoid** (or Europeans) and **Mongoloid** (or Asians).

What percentage Sub-Saharan DNA is shared ancestry DNA with so-called African Americans, proven are actually Nubian Americans? Answer is a walloping **14%!!!** Are all people descendants of Black people? The facts support a correct **"yes,"** and not any theory or conjecture by the experts in the area of learning; that causes a great deal of discomfort to those believing in "<u>White</u> <u>Supremacy</u> <u>Fraud</u>" of any kind. Because there's only "one race," the human race **"One Specie."** **God bless all Americans** especially at her bottom, poor **Nubian Americans.** This validates & answers a Nubian American census question, that's a "national confirmation."

Incidentally before we go, if you was wondering what **Goshen** meant, it's a region of ancient Egypt, east of the Nile delta; granted to Jacob and his Black **Israelite** descendants by the king of Egypt and inhabited by them until the Exodus (Genesis 45:10) for generations of children a place of comfort and plenty. The original Black Hebrew settlement located along the fringe where the delta farmland meets the eastern desert.

In Biblical names **Goshen** is: **"Approaching, drawing near"** just as the risen acceptance **soon,** of the Nubian American view of reality history that was **"Hidden"** to make this country a White nation alone; separated between two great oceans to experiment with freedoms aside (out of the way) from God to have complete control of others. Perhaps, America is todays "big-bro" **Israel.**

In human genetics, the White (Caucasian) race is derived from haplogroup R is a Y-chromosome DNA haplogroup, subgroup of haplogroup P, defined by the M207 mutation. The "American Dream," expressed as happiness through material wealth, was never intended for Nubian Americans. We reject historical brainwashing wherein white society teaches falsely that Nubian Americans were savages who were civilized through slavery and accomplishments that were Nubians instead were white. This falsity of white history originated and ends with their desire to hide their true nature on a fabricated concept that has become **dangerously** delusional.

America is an example of democracy achieved for whites only, even after **Nubian American slaves** built it. Absolute power sets the stage for absolute evil. Whiteness has set the standard in America that's soon in changing as a fact, **"nothing remains the same."** Nubian Americans will rise again, aspire to "prominence & power" as **Biblical scriptures foreseen with prophesy...** And above everything else, it is our **job** and **duty,** at the *Fortney Encyclical History Ed. Co.* to *elevate* and *assent* the *Nubian American cause;* with these lessons of the *real story* implicitly of *facts,* with God's truth in *evidence* and let it fall where it may; to *thwart* other's misleading **depicted** evilness in history against God's *true image* **"The Black Man,"** (without instituting black racism of any kind), only with knowledge, understanding and it's *wisdom to all.*

AFFIDAVIT NUBIAN AMERICAN IDENTITY: Census Appendix

"Labels & Titles" were intentionally given just to give us a demeaning status, of a once enslaved people as property. Black American's are not generationally less human beings. Our heritage ties us to identify, as **Nubian American.** Describes a kinky wooly-haired Black person's ethnicity and race, from other parts of the world other than Africa. For example, a person may identify as a Black African and some with straight hair, like Asian Blacks of India's people with black-skin. However, the kinky wooly-hair declaration distinguishes between the two (once made fun of in White man's Jim Crow era), however **"Hair-Power $$$"** is now very important.

"Diversity" is dissolving race into **"identity."** Euro-America was fully aware, but hid from us in their education of learning, of our **Africa Nubia's** kinky wooly-hair identity in education; just as they used whitewashing Cleopatra in Black Egypt's Africa, and Black history they worked so hard to cover-up with extreme measures. Their deception was, try making her pure white wearing "Klan" suites as historian scholars, with "white privilege supremacy" a cause.

What Cleopatra fought hard to **preserve** was Egypt is Black Africa, like wooly-hair Blacks here as **Nubian Americans.** At the least, if an add-mixture of 30% to even 50% outside Egyptian but by white people's one-drop own standards, makes you a Black human being. Allowing false depicted history, has a rippling effect of harming. To exclude Nubian American identity is to exclude Cleopatra being black, the Bible explaining the black Jesus Christ, of Europe and South American's Black Madonna's Christ, and all of black history as **falsely** "white."

White man's creation of lying with racism, **controls** indigent blacks to an extent "life and death" indirectly saying, he's the creator of civilization with alien workers such as slaves or now space beings other than earth! Racist historian belief says, if **Nubia History** is allowed, it refutes, goes against and exposes all Euro-U.S.A. school-house histories that were lies, with whitewashed claims of all **North Africa** to **Israel.** And so, **identifying** the Nubian American had to be omitted in white man's world history. However, endeavors of today's Nubian American has risen to America's surface, for confirmation census. Thank you.

Our Precious Children

Money goes for cheap labor, jobs going overseas. Our black children shouldn't grow-up in despair, needing a partner collision to 'do for self,' to own our own economic culture. Things are bad but in 'unity' there is always strength.

3,000 Years Old Helicopter, Submarine ETC.

ABU SIMBEL TEMPLES complex: A miracle carved in the mountains that date back to Ramses II, 13th century BC are in **Nubia**, and wrongly depicted many times in history as in Egypt is our books cover. However, a **3,000 years old helicopter, submarine** etc. (above) is above an entrance of the Egyptian **Temple of Seti I.**

The Sacred Black Madonna

The sacred Black Madonna of Jasna Gora according to traditional history, was painted by the Gospel Maker Luke. It is said Luke drew 'two' Madonnas, and that one of these is in Czestochowa. We in America do not know, that when the Polish Pope each time he returns to Poland visits the shrine there, of the Virgin of Czestochowa or The Black Madonna, the first virgin and Black Child, wo later evolved into Mary and Jesus, before becoming WHITE with the help of Michelangelo, between 1508 and 1512 at the commission of Pope Julius II who was a "warrior pope" who in an aggressive campaign for political control to unite and empower Italy under the leadership of the church. A copy of the "Translario tabulae" dating from 1474 is kept in me archives of the monastery Jasna Gora. According to scholarly version, the picture was originally a Black Byzantine icon of the "Hodegerria," "she who shows the way," from between the 6th and the 9th century. Judaism rejects that Jesus was the awaited Messiah, prophecies in the Tanakh. In Islam, Jesus (Arabic translation is Isa) is considered an important prophet of God, of a virgin birth, worker of miracles. Islam and the Baha'l faith, title "Messiah" for Jesus.

Akebu-Lan means "Mother of Mankind" Map

Akebu-Lan is the oldest and means "Mother of Mankind" or "Garden of Eden," was used by the Moors, Nubians, Numidians, Khart-Haddans (Carthagenians), and the name Africa was given to this continent by the Romans. In 1,675 B.C. neither the name Jew nor Negro existed. The term Negro was given to the Blacks as they left Africa for slave ships 1,500 A.D. when the name "Negroland" was used. This term coined by the Portuguese meant "black." This term saved the slave traders having to identify each slave whether he was a Cushite, Ethiopian, or a Abyssinian, sometimes called in the bible. England and Portugal knew well these peoples whom they captured and chained, many times helped by ambitious Arabs, were the first ones to carry and establish Christianity and Judaism in Africa, northeast Africa, and Europe. Western bias whites have so foiled, baffled, defeated and blocked the history of the 'Black Race' so extensively, that it takes great study and research to 'unravel' his maze of myths, pictorial lies and confusion.

The Ancient Connection of Northeast Africa

This map gives the ancient connection of continental Africa to the neighboring northeastern land mass. Students, black folks and unknowing Americans have been led to believe by Western historians that Havilah (Arabia), Ethiopia, and Assyria (Mesopotamia), Persia, and Syria were separate and disconnected in their historical and geographical context, however, during biblical times they were very much connected. Since the river Niel flowed from southern Ethiopia and emptied into the Great Sea (Mediterranean) people migrated from lower Africa and journeyed to Northeast Africa (Canaan, Palestine) or today's Israel. There was no body of water to separate the two. The Suez Canal wasn't dug until the 19th century. And during War II war correspondents began to refer to North Africa and Northeast Africa as the "Middle East." The term "Middle East" disrespected by white required no need mention of Africa hence, avoid giving black recognition!

AFFIDAVIT NUBIAN AMERICAN IDENTITY: Appendix
Conclusion

It is what it is but why, was the back-bone nation's fundamental foundation of great Africa's **pre-history;** *"world's first statue monuments"* carved in *mountainous* **stone** as evidence and in fact, was a Sudan Nubian **Nubia's** civilization whose rulers built **cities** isn't taught to us? Learnt was "Egypt & Mesopotamia" they did a job-on whitewashing; but dared-tamper in Nubia, Africa's, **"The Nubian Gateway"** where rich deposits of **gold,** ivory, incense and ebony wood from Sub-Saharan Africa were **traded,** to Egypt and civilizations throughout the Mediterranean; and for about 100 years **conquered** and ruled Egypt's 25th Dynasty. They knew they couldn't cover-up was deliberately bye-passed; by a racist historian's threat, to **Nubian American's** world history.

Now here's where the evil and **"racist hate"** comes in at. They've been **taught** as a child, to take a black man's **life** doesn't matter; especially a racist white-police, who **gets away** with it!!! They think we're "nothing," until they learn **kinky-hair Nubian Americans** are the same **pre-history** people whose ancestors had a civilization, whose rulers built temples; while white racist at the same time like any animal living in **caves,** had no intellect, a must be known to them. And claiming white supremacy, doesn't remove an **uncivilized cave-man savage** instinct. **"Racism,"** is destroying the world; ever since they created it some 600 years ago. However, when **Nubian American's Rise,** America will be **saved** to go to her **Black Israel's "chosen people"** prophesy...

Just like, the ancient over 2,000 years old **"Baghdad Dry Cell Batteries,"** a Euro-U.S. & Jew's unbelievable, in envy perhaps but "not **forgotten,**" by bigot sophisticated scholars of deceptions ready-made policy of a racist society. It didn't fit in with the mainstream established viewpoint, who hoped would go away like **mixing** Israel did. Electricity was made out a pottery jar, copper sheet, vinegar the likely acid, asphalt, and an iron electrode. And **Israel** is not <u>white-Jews</u> **home.**

Just like chiseled in **stone,** the temple of Seti I's hieroglyphs in **Abydos,** black **Kemet** (Egypt), **3,000 years old** ancient helicopter, submarine and airplanes depicting "modern-tech." or the monumental **Nubian "first"** world figures, carved out of mountainous stone (Mount Rushmore <u>imitated</u>), is **Abu Simbel,** "The Rock Temple in **Nubia** (Cush)," are about **pre-histories legacies of rulers.** Ancient **Nubian's** better way of life **lessons;** is *that old kind religion,* will heal & inspire   economics "growth & prosperity" for the *struggling* is the **Nubian American identity,** a today's **census registry.** A *Fortney Encyclical History Ed. Co.'s,* "Thank You."

"WE ARE PROVEN NUBIAN AMERICANS"

To begin with, at a news conference in December of 1988 at Chicago's Hyatt Regency O' Hare Hotel, it was said leaders of "75 black groups" met, and with Rev. Jessy Jackson, a new national black agenda of being called "African American," was accomplished.

The Rev. Jessy Jackson said, "To be called African-Americans has cultural integrity," "it puts us in our proper "historical context;" then most certainly, what more when historical context describe cultural heredity identity..." There's no limit with more that define as being **"Nubian Americans,"** and what it does to a certain **"tribal nation"** of people distinguished by their important trait of physicality; and that being **kinky wooly-hair** like **lamb's wool** and skin like **burnt bronze,** biblical description is today's **Nubian Americans** whites hate to give recognition.

If a national survey, the polls would likely show their great numbers with **dignity** and **pride,** what Black peoples want to be called is **Nubian Americans** is their **"heritage"** from the **African Continent.** This the new term to replace the <u>African</u> <u>Americans</u> term, with the preferred Nubian Americans acceptance; among doubters opinion makers there's Africa's Nubia **DNA, that will quite any objections,** a powerful imagery of a political exercise in naming, to the national press. We recalled the imposition of "Black" over "Negro," then became "African American," now a recall to become called, a Nubian American's **"proper world-wide known identity."**

We redefine ourselves, Nubian Americans to gain back our ancient **pre-history** ancestors just do respect and to educate the today's <u>racist</u> <u>hate</u> <u>society,</u> that destroys with <u>evil</u> and <u>kills</u> the unarmed innocent black-man. Has held us to be an <u>inferior</u> random and <u>sub</u>-<u>human</u> to their <u>white</u> <u>supremacy</u> <u>agenda</u>, it almost seems, allowing title-tags without specific identity to be the norm. Reconstruction era as humiliating and even vengeful imposing to them and not wanted.

Recently, hundreds of news organizations have changed back to a Black tag in reference to the old struggle and race of us kinky wooly-hair people who trace their ancestry to Africa; strikes deeper to Nubian Americans who were <u>stripped</u> of their "<u>bye-passed</u> identity" and <u>enslaved</u>. Denied of speaking their motherland tongue of Nubian, who were known worldwide in **"trading."** We now pay homage to a recall, a rightfully deserved that people **"gains,"** many Nubian Americans has shed their **blood** for.

This asks an important question, but what is white historians excuse for <u>bypassing,</u> <u>over</u>-<u>looking</u> and just plain **"<u>hiding</u>,"** knowledge from all American student's education, of Nubian history who once ruled in ancient Egypt? Would greatly lessen stupidity or help to eliminate his <u>racist's</u> doings. **Nubia,** is home to civilization's older than the dynastic Egyptians, evade the Nile River in what is today's northern **Sudan** and southern Egypt was purposely paid relatively little attention. However, Nubian history is often intertwined with Egypt's to the north.

<u>Racism</u>, and/is a rediscovery by Nubian Americans of Ancient Nubia even to the architect of the pyramid. Although different in statue and build and created earlier than the famed great Egyptian pyramids of Giza, Sudan has more pyramids than Egypt. There are around **2,000** Kushite (Cushite Nubian) pyramids in upper Sudan, compared with 200 Egyptian pyramids. Hence, Nubian history was <u>ignored</u> because it was not European white-man's history like <u>whitewashed</u> Egypt is.

Plus, due to the **fact,** that <u>racist</u> archaeologist and <u>bigoted</u> white historians actually <u>dismissed</u> the idea of black Africans were capable of creating anything artistic, of technology, or cities like those from Egypt, Greece or Rome. Nubia's **Negroes,** were a mere extension of Egypt with a few paragraphs on black pharaohs at best, if that much. We will no longer tolerate, **wrong!!!**

Nubian study, a "magnificent historical significance," for **Nubian Americans** and all other students for *high learning* was <u>rejected,</u> for <u>white</u> <u>supremacy</u> control in power, with the <u>fear</u> of a black-people take over aggression. However, **Africa's** history emphatically says, **Ethiopia** is the *"Grandmother,"* **Nubia** the *"Mother"* and **Egypt** is the *"child."* This is the **"beginning"** of all of civilization's history, no matter how they the <u>outsider</u> try to <u>distort,</u> a beautiful honest *"Truth."*

Black, was the common understanding until Europeans painted Biblical characters **white;** to able him without <u>hateful</u> <u>envy</u> in <u>spite</u> to worship them, and not the **"spirit of God;"** having everyone glorify and praise the white man as if God, because he couldn't in "God's" true image. Ham had a son named **Cush,** which means **black** in **Hebrew.** Cush is the most common usage designating color, referring to people, persons or lands used in the Bible. It is used **"58 times"** in the King James Version. The Greek/Latin word is **Ethiopia.** In classical literature, **Greek** and **Roman** authors describe Ethiopians as "Black."

The Nubia DNA can be explained in Genesis 10:6-20 that describes the descendants of ham as being located in North, Central, South Africa and southern **Asia.** Psalm 105:23 mentions the "Land of Ham" in Egypt, and Psalm 78:51 connects the "tents of Ham" with Egypt. In Genesis 10, Nimrod, son of Cush, whose name means black, founded a civilization in **Mesopotamia.** The Egyptians (Ham), are **"genetically"** linked to **Sub-Saharan**

Nubians. The **Romans** record that there were "Black People" in **Britain** (White Man's prehistory) and other parts of Europe, when they first encountered them.

"ANCIENT NUBIAN 6,000 YRS. OLD GOLD ECONOMICS STUDY"

Ancient 6,000 years old economics of the Nubian gold trade alone, should have promulgated, is a spearheaded histories top of the list need; for **K-12 Nubian History Schoolhouse Learning** in education that to the south of Egypt was "Rich and Powerful **Nubia**;" and not excluded, built on the **devil's** advocate of "**white supremacy's** fraud and fear." Not only is racist hate attacks killing innocent **"Nubian Americans,"** has killed by erasing Nubian history from our minds except relayed coming from "Kings and Queens." We will **"rise"** soon, what we attempt with the topic of Nubia's **ancient gold,** like Nubian Christ's eternal glorious **resurrection...**

Just as, now we learn, through the gold trade's **6,000 years,** that **Nubian** history is before the mistaken **Sumerians.** Our golden history, relates to the **Nile River** (the Gihon river as known in the Holy Bible), that goes through Uganda, the Sudan, and extends from northern Kenya to the Mediterranean Sea is a total of **3,485 miles.** The **longest** river, "in the world." Just as the so-called Middle-East (Asia Minor), is actually of the Nubian Continent's, **"Northeast Africa."**

A once one land mass, before the [so-called] disconnect digging of the Suez Canal in 1869. And the region of Mesopotamia, which included Assyria and **Babylonia** (Iraq is now located), were the original jet black **"Hamites and Shemites,"** also, Hebrew original **black Jews.** The name of Jesus in Hebrew is **Ye-shu-ah,** which means, "one who shall save by righteous teachings and example" (Matthew 3:15).

Ancient 6,000 years of gold mining in the Eastern Deserts of Egypt and Nubia/Sudan are located in the crystalline basement east of the Nile and primarily bound to quartz veins. Nubia, particularly rich in gold deposits, was an important envied conquest for the ancient Egyptians. **"Gold mines,"** which some of them were under Egyptian control can be proven in **Nubia.** Gold bearing quartz chunks due to erosion were collected by hundreds of workers, then processed in Wadis dry valleys of the mountains. They call it, "wadiworkings."

Ancient Nubia's location was so ideal for trade. The Nile River was the route to Egypt and rich port cities circumference of the Mediterranean Sea. Ancient Nubia had access in the east to the Red Sea, opening up trade to the Arabian Peninsula, the southern east coast of Africa and ports farther away. By the time of Egypt's First Dynasty, **international trade** was with regions of the Levant (Israel), Libya, and Nubia. Egypt had a trading colony in Canaan, a number of them in Syria, but even more in **Nubia.** The overland trade route was through the Wadi Hammamat from the Nile to the Red Sea, then goods traveled on the "backs of donkeys."

Many of these trade agreements were achieved through peaceful negotiation, and some were established by military campaigns on both sides. Nubia was rich in gold mines and gets its name in fact, from the Egyptian word for gold, **Nub.** There were many trade centers in Nubia however, one of the most important of them referred to in Egyptian text was **"Yam."** During the Old Kingdom of Nubia (2613-2118 BC), Yam was noted for its **ebony** hard wood (reddish brown and black), **ivory,** and **gold,** location of Yam precisely is unknown however, it is thought to have been somewhere in the **"Shendi Reach"** area of the Nile River in modern-day **Sudan.**

Cush's (Nubia) location and natural resources made it an important trading junction or a center. Ancient Nubia linked central and southern Africa to Egypt. Black Egyptian Pharaohs sent expeditions on ships south along the Nile River to buy, or sometimes a <u>raid</u> to <u>steal</u>, goods. But however the deal, Egyptians traded wheat grain and linen cloth for Nubian's precious gold, ivory, leather, and timber.

During Byzantine times, the **Bedouin tribes,** who dominated the entire Eastern Desert as tradition would have it, were not interested in mining (still are today), refused any kind of digging in the ground; even agriculture in watered, Wadi grounds. However in contrast, in Northeast Sudan away from areas close to the Nile River, many new sites were started in secondary gold deposits of Wadi working operations.

Of all the many known Pharaonic gold producing sites in Egypt and Northeast Sudan, the history surely about 6,000 years tradition in gold producing, however, less than the monthly output of gold was achieved of present day South Africa; which was still a lot of gold back then.

The total tonnage of all mined ancient trenches and underground operations was estimated to the order of 400,000 to 600,000 tons of quartz ore. Figuring a recovery of 10 grams/a ton, is about 2/3rd the maximum concentration mined, a maximum of 6,000 kilograms of Au grade is yielded. One kg (kilogram) of gold ='s 1,000 9 (grams), and today's 1 kilo ='s 2.2 pounds or $59,372.8 x 6,000 kilos is $356,236 **million** dollars times 5 the value at least the ancient past; ='s 1 trillion, 881 billion, 180 million, 000, 000 dollars or $1,881,180,000,000 dollars **"6,000 years ago,** that lasted about, almost a **thousand** years.

As Egypt became bigger they desired much more **"luxury goods"** such as **gold, animal skins, gemstones** and **perfumes.** They established a trade relationship with ancient Nubia to obtain gold the Egyptians needed for more exotic wood and Nubians needed grain to survive, the Egyptians had. And besides other

African Kingdoms and Arabia, Nubia also traded with distant **Rome,** of Italy, **India,** and even **China.** The largest, wealthy ancient Nubian city of **Meroe,** was the hub, a center metropolis of Cushite civilization and gold trade at its height, lasted just about a **1,000 years.** Nubian shield hosted around **250 gold mine** production **sites.**

And so today, with this blatant "white-supremacy" lie, and replacement theory running ramped, in America, no wonder anyone can clearly see why monumental statues of beautiful **"Nubian Kings and Queens,"** (many with wide nose and thick lips chipped away), and the magnificently carved **"Rock Temple of Abu Simbel,"** was meant to be absent, by bigoted Euro-Americans who avoided **Nubian** history. And brazenly, falsely-depicted as Egyptian; posing as the architect creator of **Africa's** "Great Pyramids," in schoolhouse studies world-history.

"GOLD," the yellow metal that captures the heart and some men souls, who'll take another's life… It is said that **gold** (money), is the "root" of all **evil.** However, there's an evil root "worst" than gold. The worst root said to be, is the worst lie ever told was there's no such thing as the **DEVIL.** And only an evil **devil**, as Nubian wooly-hair **Christ** emphasized the proof is in John 8:44, "Ye are of *your* father the devil…a liar and the father of it." Would lie and make it appear the scriptures great Cush (Nubian nation), the **first man** on earth was of **black skin** and **wooly hair** made in **God's image,** was the ones who **created** and **wrote** the **Holy Bible;** that their superb history **never existed!** Nubian history is **left-out** of white man's world history.

Not in any racist sense, but we were God's "chosen people" who'll return to **Israel** and not a people who fake to be us Rev. 2:9, "…say they are Jews, and are not, but *are* the synagogue of Satan." This is astutely recognized, and pointed-out with no harm intended; in a provocative positive sense, only to inspire. **Nubian Africa's "black man's golden-history,"** wrote the **Bible** that European whites <u>revised</u>. They depict with <u>racist</u> <u>overtones,</u> all major original kinky wooly hair black characters in text book study and **Hollywood's** Jewish owned filming industry; they've <u>whitewashed</u> as all white, except always with us as <u>demeaning</u> <u>servants</u> or <u>slaves</u> are the **"black Africans** or **Nubian Americans."**

The grand historian author of the *Fortney Encyclical History Ed. Co.,* is bent on everyone having the correct knowledge with learning and an honest **understanding** and **"lessons of wisdom,"** from an array of our company books. The future is our precious children. We must teach & instruct all our children at an early age; by showing them a pattern to live by not acting the <u>fool</u>, but in the **right**-way for peace and harmony, for all races to live together and **co-exist.**

We together must take care of this **planet,** it's the only one we have to live on. Because it's a known fact of death that, no worldly goods and no amount of **gold** or money can you take with you, once leaving here forever. And so, having nowhere else to go we must all clean the earth, water, and air from pollutants, but most of all our **"minds"** from the pollutants of <u>hate</u> and <u>racism</u> toward a more **righteous thinking,** whatever your spiritual belief.

Nubia Region Today Map

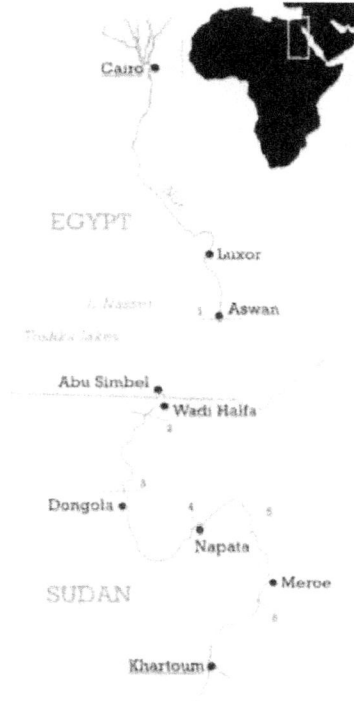

Nubia was also called - Upper & Lower Nubia, Kush, Land of Kush, Te-Nehesy, Nubadae, Napata, or the Kingdom of Meroe.

The region referred to as Lower Egypt is the northernmost portion. Upper Nubia extends south into Sudan and can be subdivided into several separate areas such as Batn El Hajar or "Belly of Rocks", the sands of the Abri-Delgo Reach, or the flat plains of the Dongola Reach. Nubia, the hottest and most arid region of the world, has caused many civilizations to be totally dependent on the Nile for existence.

Nubian Meroe Pyramids

Ramesses II Storming the Hittite Fortres of Dapur.
Meroe people were Kushite, Nubia who rule 25th
Dynasty Egypt

The Great Nubian is Before the Egyptians

**The Giza plateau 3 predominant Pyramids & Great Sphinx
Lower left, The Great Sphinx face east**

25th Nubian Dynasty/Kushite Tadja made of Ivory 760-656BC

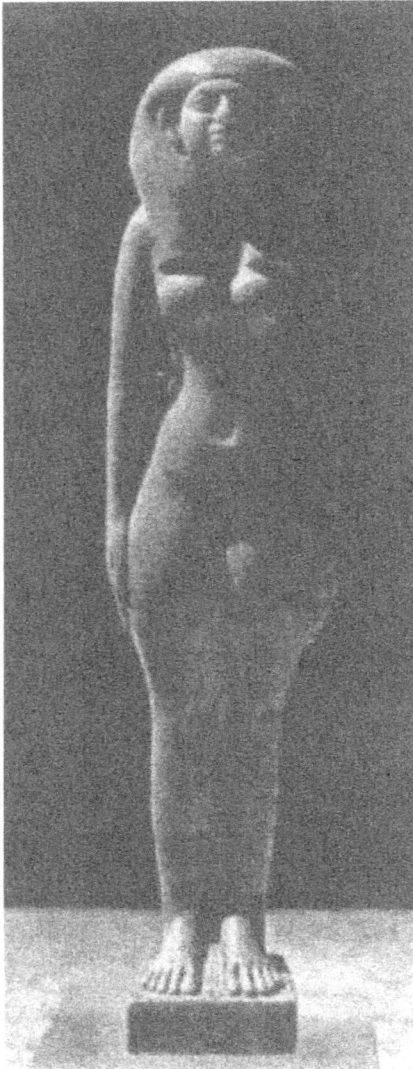

Nubian Winged Goddess 743-712BC Earthenware

"WOLLY-HAIR CHRIST WAS A BLACK NUBIAN"

Nubian American's great Africa's past, cannot be hidden or chipped away wide black nose and beautiful thick lips in white man's "envy explorations" to <u>steal</u> land, religion and history in the name of **"<u>evil</u>."** And with, <u>anti-black</u> <u>hate-groups</u> in fear of losing their **<u>white-supremacy</u> <u>lie</u>** along with their "<u>replacement theory</u>" excuse to *practice* **"<u>genocide</u>"** on others, brings to light the "motherland of humanity" is the sacred black color of **Africa,** and her Black form of **God** is only **natural;** welcomed **"rediscovery"** of our **Nubian American selves.** Because to "love a White version" of our Black God of Christ, is to *subconsciously* <u>despise</u> or <u>hate</u> your Black-self.

A shrine to the **Black Madonna** and the **Prince of peace,** is the word **Christ,** comes from Indian, Krishna or Chrishna, which means "the Black one." The Egyptian God Osiris, the Krishnas of India; the Buddhas of India, Japan and China; the Xaha of Japan; Laotsze of China; the Fuhi of China; the Sommonacom of Siam; the ancient Druid gods; and the gods of Greece were **Black.** Black Grecia gods included were Apollo, Baccus, Jupiter, Hercules, and Ammon; and the goddesses Isis, Venus Junno, Metis, Hecati, Cybele and Ceres were all worshipped in Rome of Italy. **<u>Original author</u> <u>of</u> <u>the</u> "<u>HOLY</u> <u>BIBLE</u>" <u>were</u> <u>kinky</u> <u>wool-hair</u> <u>African</u> <u>Nubians</u>.**

A white Christ encourages subservience of Black people to whites, who occupy most all Americans political seats of authority, and the Nubian American is our model only we can embody correctly, ours without fault of **identity.** Blackness is an *"essence"* structure of realities **"first."** Because, a Black people who allow white others to determine their image with a white God will allow and go for anything of others to "control" our women and children, goods, economic resources, and necessities of Black lives. **Images always go much deeper than words.**

Do not fear Black Christ. Perhaps **Hollywood's** objective, with **dark** looking **devils** or **black monsters** looking human like in their movies; that sub-consciously *all children minds* will fear Black-people, are **"genocide hate set-ups,"** with **monster movies; Satan's** *reverse* tricknology; whites conveniently always looking right on screen. And sub-consciously, many black women may burn in hell; an abomination of longing to be in the arms of an evil deceptive, and made-up blond hair, blue eyes idol, with an "All American white Christ," was the **Slave-master's** *dream* of reasoning; with psycho-sexual analytic theories, for his experimenting **breeding** farms.

Just as or like, the **"Great Wall of China,"** was built in the 14th through the 17th centuries A.D. during the Ming Dynasty and when European 15th century **"racism was created."** However, if China told it like it is, was to keep the trouble-makers, the northern-white nomadic tribes out of China from **invasion.** Most-likely China through trading with Nubian/Egyptians, were warned by either or both to keep them out. Build a wall, like we didn't have the chance too, perhaps hinted to China who kept in mind and did. What remains was mostly built in the Ming Dynasty (1368-1644). The average height is 20 to 23 feet tall, and the tallest section of the wall was 46 feet. The length of the great wall is **13,170.70** miles long. America's coast to coast is 3,100 miles.

Then there's the notion, perhaps China contemplated and saw what happened to **Africa's** Black Israelite **Jews,** by Whites who **say they are Jews and are not.** Said, **"The liberator Christ."** And so, whatever it was, China decided and built her great wall on speculation or without, ever done in history, to keep an enemy out of China. Their anticipation was certain, and built with spaced watch-towers on top the wall to communicate any approach of the menace they feared, known to have a troubling history. A renowned white man once said, "Strong fences makes for good neighbors." And so, **proud** "new neighbors" are always **Nubian Americans. Amen.**

The dictionary definition of African American is "an American of Africa and especially of Black African descent;" but no important word such as **Nubian,** much less Nubian American is in any dictionary print... Then next, there's the word **"Afro:"** a hairstyle of tight curls in a full evenly rounded shape. White man's dictionary skipped over *global nickname* **Nubian** to Afro!

However, there is a term that truly describes with all kinds of proof, (aside from school-book learning), a people who were taken from Africa and forced into slavery and that term is properly called identity; which describes the unique kinky wooly-hair black-skin of distinction is the **"Nubian American;"** is the correction and not the African American per-se (as such). The term **"Nubia"** means to the many *"world-wide"* and *"in America,"* **it has come to be virtually synonymous with *"Blackness"* and *Africa.*" Cush** (Nubia) is mentioned **"58" times** in the Bible.

In conclusion, Isaiah 18:2, referred the **Cushites** (Nubians) as a people "feared near and far," and a "nation mighty and conquering." This was the ancient **Nubian** (Cushite) "military reputation," in ancient Egypt and the Near East for the most part. It is also important to note: **Cush** (Kush), **Ethiopic** Nubians, **Sudanic** Nubians and **Egyptic** Nubians are same *stock* **"Nubia people's"** DNA military might, but also a **"land of wealth"** known for its *"precious stones."* Job mentions the *topaz* of Cush as being very valuable (Job 28:19). **"Israelite people's identity"** was **defined** by its relationship to **Yahweh (Christ),** the **God of**

Israel. But not in **history** books?

Cush will experience Yahweh's **judgment** (Amos 9:8). The Bible is clear that **Nubia** [Cush's descendants, the Nubian Americans], are like ancient **Israel** [today's Palestinians and Nubians] who also will experience Christ's **salvation** (Zephaniah 3:10) and (Psalms 68:31), that was prophesized. America's Statue of Liberty and its relationship **"warnings,"** of Babylon (Rev. 17:1 to 18). **"Repent" America, do your job and "Rise" together with God's Nubian Americans!**
Nubian American Means Black Creativity. *"The mark of distinction."* Let's get *smarter* about *us.*

We would like to congratulate your book **"The Fortney Encyclical Black History: The World's True Black History"** as it has been appraised. From traditional publishers, they have given a promising **8.2** out of **10.** Although there remark is slightly confidential, you may be pleased to know that this is what the reviewers have said, *"The author weaves words together like a fine thread formulating ideas, relating scenes or images together exceptionally. The voice is pronounced and consistent, which is vital in any celebrated literary piece. These are the qualities that set the author apart from all other writers."* I hope you realize that this is exceptional material. It has captivated literary agents and, surely its future readers. A Senior Book Agent & Brand Manager from Scriptor House.

A **"Racial Standard with Hair"** is that, there's an emphasis concerning hair and the races we just can't ignore in closing. We start with the **Asian** Continent of **India's** black-skin people having **"straight"** black hair. Then there's the **Spanish Latino** very light brown-skin people having **"straight"** black hair. Then there's the **Chinese Asian** [so-called by Euro-historians] yellow-skin people having **"straight"** black hair. However, then there's the **African** largest continent of black-skin people **Nubian African** and the **North Americas Nubian American "kinky wooly"** black-hair distinction; are the only people or anywhere else let it be known, even with skin as light or lighter than brown people's skin, are the "only ones" who can claim this unique type hair in the world. *The Planet is On Fire…Climate-Change at point of no return!*

White man scholars of history can't <u>imitate</u> to follow-up or resemble as a model with **kinky wooly hair** to <u>whitewash</u> <u>history,</u> even after <u>chipping</u>-<u>away</u> black's big lips and wide noses of Nubian/Egyptians ancient representing statues and monument. And so, he <u>completely</u> **omitted** Nubia/Cush from **his false** 'world history and dictionary's.' Please note there are some original Ethiopians next door neighbors to Nubia with genetically straight hair; believed in prehistory migrated and settled as India's Asian beginning. This makes **"Kinky Wooly Hair"** having the important and vital, racial standard with a **"Hair's Mark of Distinction"** of a people.

We all know, if not can feel or heard what the White man's standard is in America that once made fun of and not in good jest but a <u>mockery,</u> of a hero unaware to Black folk. However, we saying in defense against that <u>mockery</u> in disguise of an **"unknowing hero."** So before we leave you, the last vital **lesson** aside from DNA, all Black folks must know that no matter how light towards White your skin, if you got our "hero" of **kinky wooly-hair** on top of your head to chin distinctively like Black skin, you **"Nubian American Family"** my brother of greatness that's in God's image what gets you in… And God bless America against White or Black <u>Racism</u> period.

"And Last But Not Least, For the Record," America can't have her cake and eat it too; you can't mix the righteous good with the <u>evil</u> bad all together and call it one with under God, and declare a freedom for its rights. God objects to His, "Biblical Rule of Laws" not up-held; with warnings to living in peaceful co-existing is either this or that; one way or the other; with no straddling the fence that "man marry woman & woman marry man" is perhaps the whole issue.

Directly from our <u>misuse</u> and <u>abuse</u> of God's **"gift of sexuality,"** stems a large percent of the world's problems that could be greatly reduced like; STD's Aids, divorce, fatherless children, incest, sex trafficking, rape etc... If **"God's"** rule of laws were "upheld and obeyed," of His sexuality standards, disease would drop immensely world-wide, economy would rise and most all mental hospitals would have empty beds if we all sought to live within the healthy practice God instructed to do. Same sex marriage **denounce God** is an <u>unthinkable</u> **evil** act in His name?

Not only to **procreate,** but vitally important **ancestral traits,** are handed down through generations such as: intelligence, mannerism, physical structural appearance, and personality. God's pleasure is real, and man and woman in marriage of coming together as one is truly satisfying; <u>Satan</u>, and his <u>devils</u> counterfeit joys of folly, is empty and <u>destructive</u> with pleasure; because **chromosome genetic traits,** are transmitted through **"God's gift"** of **sexual pleasure** in **marriage** when "sperm meets egg as one." *Woman* is *part* of *man* making them *one* in *marriage*.

This is God's most outstanding rule of law in *"nature;"* protected with His stern <u>penalties</u> regardless; to those that anything other, support <u>blasphemy</u> liberty; an **atheistic** <u>mockery</u> idea to an <u>ungodly</u> freedom under democracy, period. <u>Same</u> <u>sex</u> <u>marriage</u> is **White man's** American creation. The last shall be first is the Nubian Americans in a turmoil wilderness America, whose ancestors created and practiced, a *"first democracy"* in **Northeast Africa's *"Nubian Empires."***

"The Bible Speaks" – 1 Peter 4:11. "America is Calling Evil...Good" Isaiah 5:20 – Woe unto them that call evil good, and good evil; that put darkness for light, and lightness for darkness; that put bitter for sweet, and sweet for bitter. Hebrews 13:4 – Marriage *is* honorable in all, and the bed undefiled: but whoremongers and adulterers God will judge. And, Isaiah 5:24. God did not make homosexuals; it is **not** a DNA genetic trait, their actions are a result of their own lust and evil desires – James 1:13-14. Sometimes forced upon one (the hell of prison). **HELP THEM!** Hebrew 13:3 – Remember them who are in prison, as though in prison with them, and them which suffer [hard times], since you also...**Same sex marriage goes against God's Black image!!**

If YOU are guilty of homosexuality and lesbianism, we urge you to be washed, be sanctified, and quit this sinful practice – Romans 1:16, Mark 16:16; Acts 2:38; 1 Corinthians 6:11. This isn't a **"religious hyperbole"** – extravagant exaggeration used as a figure of speech, just to influence; this is truth, honor, integrity, with liberty and salvation is **"Real LOVE to Live By with SOUL."**

America is somewhat like, biblical **Babylon.** The setting of the **Holy Bible** all took place in **Northeast Africa,** despite political constructs of so-called (originated in America) Middle East and western Asia. They don't want to credit Black-skinned people with *"intelligence,"* a <u>racist</u> agenda. And the Bible does not differentiate race; it only differentiates **nationalities** and **tribes. Acts 17: 26 And hath made of one blood all nations of men...** *Nubians are Gods chosen people.*

Today's **<u>fascist</u>** right wing conservative's ideology called "Trump Republicans," seem to have as nature's DNA characteristic, with a negative **<u>evil</u>** genetic trait. <u>Racist White-Supremacist</u> modern-day **<u>Satan</u>** was Hitler, now is protégé **<u>Satan</u>** Trump, to **<u>anti</u>-<u>Christ</u>** Putin then America's Republican Senate

coup with a dangerous **demonic** ideology, won't change with bad laws that:

1. You want kids to have weapons of mass destruction, as a **demand** of your **oath** of office??
2. You **kicked** God out of our schools, now why you want kids **raped** to have the children??
3. You want climate change that's destroying the planet earth is a global **EMERGANCY**.
4. You want **"lies"** that can take the lives or kill black and brown to dominate the House & Senate with the courts that also threatens. With **unaccountable** racist white police killings of blacks with nothing done but frivolous investigations lead to no prosecution, as justice.
5. You want laws to gerrymander the vote and ruin democracy, and control all evil sorts of **power**. You're America's creator of *same sex marriage* a *right* to an *evil oath*, under **God**??
6. You want your knee to continue strangling on the necks of the poor, pay high taxes while the wealthy corporations pay nothing expanding their gluttonous **'profit'** practices. Satan Semite with no empathy no mercy **beware** biting **you,** creating a **blackman** devil's **wrath.**
7. You reject law enforcement accountability to racist acts that kill black and brown people. With some **police** secretly acting out, within the benevolent association in **cowardice** to **murder,** and conspire in a secret unspoken oath, to pagan sacrilegious sacrificing of even children, much less black people is standard ritual for them and their **Satanic-cult/coup**.
8. You want Nubian Americans kept in a form of servitude without resource power.

9. You want the Black man's **Nubian** American's *"cultural and ancestral heritage history,"* taught in education continued being inexcusably <u>denied</u> is <u>pure</u> <u>evil</u> that may be <u>criminal</u>.

While Democracy advocates godly good DNA genetic characteristics that **must stop** the <u>lies,</u> <u>destruction</u> and <u>death</u> like todays **"<u>Satan's</u> <u>Little</u> <u>Israel;</u>"** in the **"Ancient Black man's Nubian Holy Land City of Jerusalem,"** with "Today's White man's <u>blasphemy</u> <u>gay</u> <u>parades</u> & <u>civil</u>-<u>war massacres</u>" to the likes of trying to make a "<u>Big</u> <u>Israel</u> <u>America</u>." As justice ignores our "jus tice" as was with a **patriate,** the **Nubian liberator** *Jesus*, who was <u>crucified</u> then and is now **"jes us."**

Truly our **'aim'** is telling about *"truth, trust* and *love,"* certainly a DNA's *identity* issue that's definitely not meant to <u>harm,</u> <u>hurt</u> nor <u>debase;</u> only relaying of **"God's"** absolute, *"messages and warnings,"* in the holy scriptures and out. Stay **mentally strong, alert** and hold-fast to the ethnic origin of the "Jews" lesson again, is **Hebrew Africa's** Black people. As the Bible indicates, it's in their Euro-Semite **nature.** It's in their DNA characteristic genetic trait as <u>liars,</u> to the death of others against all other **better** tribes and nations; explains why, "I know thy works… I *know* the blasphemy of them which say they are Jews, and are not, but *are* the <u>synagogue</u> of <u>Satan</u>.

"It can't be emphasized enough, that the issues of human diversity "racial differences," is only "0.1 percent." Racial differences, didn't even exist prior to Caucasians using various color codes to create a societal hierarchy (persons arrange in a grade series), that was during "The Middle Ages" renaissance so-called artistic period (created the <u>racist</u> skin-color of differences) of the 15th century. Ancient Nubians nor Egyptians never referred to one another as "black," or "brown," or "white." People were just people and the color difference **"like from the gods,"** didn't matter. People were judged solely by the content of their character, deeds and **tribal** culture or **nationhood.** This means there was **No** race or color associated with people.

But, by dividing people into various shades, Caucasian and Jews practice a "divide and rule" or **conquer method.** Just like with the new **"outer-space alien"** intervention into ancient history, use as a **method** to "undermine" hiding behind their created **"artistic license law,"** just because you can with **"Hollywood filming"** and at the head of the **"boards of education,"** won't rectify no restriction laws is just **wrong** and **"reveals"** *what* they truly are! To know who they are go to **John 8:44,** that speaks of his father the devil, the lusts he will do, he was a murderer, adode not in truth a liar and the father of it. However, *who* they truly are is in **Rev. 2:9,** all the best to you.

And so, this is their way to erase history that attacks and offend **Nubian American awareness,** divide with an undefined African American **title** (a rank, designation) is not **identity.** Just as **"Jew"** is their **"created title"** and not their true, original **identity** (the fact of being the same person or thing as claimed). By being **Euro**-Semite is proof enough of their Hebrew **fakery;** and not Biblical **Abraham's** Hebrew Nubian **stock** (Family, original), which is **"The Land of the Gods"** that even includes "Biblical Northeast Africa's **Israel**," was once a part of the continent **Africa. "Reach-out, be kind and care more for each other."** You don't have to love but respecting each other's history is mandatory to co-exist! *"History gonna be made over."*

The majority of Black and most White folks, are **ignorant** to the **"facts"** and don't have any basic knowledge, don't know about the **NUBIAN AMERICAN** Black man or Black peoples true history; or essential things for both to get along is purposely kept from them knowing, *is **Satan**.* Racism along with the White Supremacy **hoax,** is a big-time money making indirect billionaires idea, scheme, **'method & sins'** of an underhanded American industry. This vital book, ***NUBIAN AMERICAN Identity Rise DNA PROOF,*** is GOD'S **"wake-up call"** to America is **REPENT,** to the only healing remedy. Stay **mentally strong** no fade-outs or **die,** **confront** the issue to **heal** it!

In the beginning, there was only the mighty black man, and almighty God created [all] in Africa, and much time went by before the white man was created but not in Africa. **Nubia** in Africa had the **Hebrew Bible,** while uncivilized and living in caves, called a **"cave man"** white **Europeans** were pagan heathens called **gentiles.** Black and White K-12 students must be taught the *same* in school that starts with **Ethiopia...** *"In the beginning,"* then **Nubia,** and *last* ancient **Egypt.** In this chronological order of **culture,** the way it actually was in history and not starting with Egypt, enabling to deceive as the white man's civilization. This is our last chance from evil hate, an EMERGANCY for **TRUTH** to **"SAVE OUR CHILDREN"** that will give the best **insight** removing "bigoted problems and obstacles" that obstruct the black students **"best interest"** to learn of **their** heritage, and not European **misgivings.** Teach ALL our precious children is first a history of *high-tech* **sciences** like a, **"Nubian Wakanda"** of **"The DNA Great Gods of Africa."**

"Nubian Americans" – Fortney Encyclical History Ed. Co.'s Grand historian author **Albert Fortney Jr.** – Sole proprietor Exec., **Ms. Cynthia Byrd** – Lovely Chief Executive Officer (C.E.O.).

The **history company** became a Fortney Encyclical History Ed. Co. in 8/01/2017; when the book, *"A Child's Short History Book – Black History Month African Study (In cartoon animal characters)"* by Albert Fortney Jr., became an international enterprise; as/for an educational [non-profit] company, when copies were sent in 12/09/2014 to **Africa's** Oprah Winfrey Academy for girls. The book is also known, sent to the state of New Jersey's Senator Honorable Mr. Cory Booker and interstate sent to Mr. Kanye West, a recognized African American entertainer.

    P.S. (Postscript), Democrat's DNA traits must fix the Supreme Court's Republican coup 6 to 3 justices advantage by expanding the court to 13, will protect the constitution in policy-making-decisions; then, the **electoral college** and the **filibuster,** both must be eliminated to protect democracy period! In order to pass a bill in the Senate, you must end the debate on it. Objecting to end the debate is called a filibuster. And 60 senators must vote to end debate, for the bill to proceed. DNA **Big Lie** is Satan father of lies Ashkenazi Jew Trump seen insurrection.

Filibuster **reform** would make it possible to pass legislation with less than 60 votes. We Nubian Americans **oppose** "filibuster reform" because it would severely backfire conveniently for "Black and Brown Progressivism," just as it already has with the 3 newly elected Supreme Court Justices Roe decision. President Mr. Biden has said he is "not a fan" of packing the court. Don't be a fan be a president and stop stalling to right the court along with House speaker Nancy Pelosi, D-Calif., told reporters that she has "no plans to bring it to the floor, " "I don't know that's a good idea…" but it's a bad and a wrong idea to just foot-dragging and loose!

    We must make sure our DNA of democracy doesn't ever again elect a candidate who loses the popular vote. The constitution assigns each state a number of *electors* based on the **"state's population."** The total number of electors is **538,** so anyone getting **"270"** of those *Electoral College votes* become *"president"* **regardless** of the popular vote.

    "Amending the constitution," requires a two-thirds vote by the House and the Senate plus approval by three-fourths of state legislatures would be too hard to get however, the *Electoral College* can become *irrelevant* **without** a constitutional amendment. Here's how: **Article 2** of the Constitution says states with a total of no less than 270 electors can agree to **"award"** all their electoral votes go to the presidential candidate who wins the **"popular vote."** And with this **automatically,** the winner of the popular vote gets the Electoral College votes to be **president**!!! Already 10 states and the District of Columbia have passed laws awarding all their electoral votes to the candidate who wins the popular vote when the 270 electoral is met.

    All together these states at present total 165 electoral say no votes. We now need additional states with 105 electoral votes agreeing to reward electoral votes to the popular vote and when that's done, never again will anyone become president who loses the popular vote. This endeavor is known as the "National Popular Vote Interstate Compact," and check to make sure your state has joined if it hasn't as yet please make sure it does! Nubian American DNA must get involved and employed in politics locally, county, state, and federal government **correct DNA education** in legislation for student's social studies history learning, with "Africa Curriculum Studies" **"colored-in with Black people's pictured history,"** and not Whites!

The
New Yorker

A Critic at Large **July 20, 2020 Issue**

The Invention of the Police

*Why did American policing get so big, so fast? The answer,
mainly, is slavery.*

By Jill Lepore
July 13, 2020

To police is to maintain law and order, but the word derives from *polis*—the Greek for "city," or "polity"—by way of *politia*, the Latin for "citizenship," and it entered English from the Middle French *police*, which meant not constables but government. "The police," as a civil force charged with deterring crime, came to the United States from England and is generally associated with monarchy —"keeping the king's peace"—which makes it surprising that, in the antimonarchical United States, it got so big, so fast. The reason is, mainly, slavery.

"Abolish the police," as a rallying cry, dates to 1988 (the year that N.W.A. recorded "Fuck tha Police"), but, long before anyone called for its abolition, someone had to invent the police: the ancient Greek polis had to become the modern police. "To be political, to live in a *polis*, meant that everything was decided through words and persuasion and not through force and violence," Hannah Arendt wrote in "The Human Condition." In the polis, men argued and debated, as equals, under a rule of law. Outside the polis, in households, men dominated women, children, servants, and slaves, under a rule of force. This division of government sailed down the river of time like a raft, getting battered, but also bigger, collecting sticks and mud. Kings asserted a rule of force over their subjects on the idea that their kingdom was their household. In 1769, William Blackstone, in his "Commentaries on the Laws of England," argued that the king, as "pater-familias of the nation," directs "the public police," exercising the means by which "the individuals of the state, like members of a well-governed family, are bound to conform their general behavior to the rules of propriety, good neighbourhood, and good manners; and to be decent, industrious, and inoffensive in their respective stations." The police are the king's men.

History begins with etymology, but it doesn't end there. The polis is not the police. The American Revolution toppled the power of the king over his people—in America, "the law is king," Thomas Paine wrote—but not the power of a man over his family. The power of the police has its origins in that kind of power. Under the rule of law, people are equals; under the rule of police, as the legal theorist Markus Dubber has written, we are not. We are more like the women, children, servants, and slaves in a household in ancient Greece, the people who were not allowed to be a part of the polis. But for centuries, through struggles for independence, emancipation, enfranchisement, and equal rights, we've been fighting to enter the polis. One way to think about "Abolish the police," then, is as an argument that, now that all of us have finally clawed our way into the polis, the police are obsolete.

B ut are they? The crisis in policing is the culmination of a thousand other failures—failures of education, social services, public health, gun regulation, criminal justice, and economic development. Police have a lot in common with firefighters, E.M.T.s, and paramedics: they're there to help, often at great sacrifice, and by placing themselves in harm's way. To say that this doesn't always work out, however, does not begin to cover the size of the problem. The killing of George Floyd, in Minneapolis, cannot be wished away as an outlier. In each of the past five years, police in the United States have killed roughly a thousand people. (During each of those same years, about a hundred police officers were killed in the line of duty.) One study suggests that, among American men between the ages of fifteen and thirty-four, the number who were treated in emergency rooms as a result of injuries inflicted by police and security guards was almost as great as the number who, as pedestrians, were injured by motor vehicles. Urban police forces are nearly always whiter than the communities they patrol. The victims of police brutality are disproportionately Black teen-age boys: children. To say that many good and admirable people are police officers, dedicated and brave public servants, which is, of course, true, is to fail to address both the nature and the scale of the crisis and the legacy of centuries of racial injustice. The best people, with the best of intentions, doing their utmost, cannot fix this system from within.

There are nearly seven hundred thousand police officers in the United States, about two for every thousand people, a rate that is lower than the European average. The difference is guns. Police in Finland fired six bullets in all of 2013; in an encounter on a single day in the year 2015, in Pasco, Washington, three policemen fired seventeen bullets when they shot and killed an unarmed thirty-five-year-old orchard worker from Mexico. Five years ago, when the *Guardian* counted police killings, it reported that, "in the first 24 days of 2015, police in the US fatally shot more people than police did in England and Wales, combined, over the past 24 years." American police are armed to the teeth, with more than seven billion dollars' worth of surplus military equipment off-loaded by the Pentagon to eight thousand law-enforcement agencies since 1997. At the same time, they face the most heavily armed civilian population in the world: one in three Americans owns a gun, typically more than one. Gun violence undermines civilian life and debases everyone. A study found that, given the ravages of stress, white male police officers in Buffalo have a life expectancy twenty-two years shorter than that of the average American male. The debate about policing also has to do with all the money that's spent paying heavily armed agents of the state to do things that they aren't trained to do and that other institutions would do better. History haunts this debate like a bullet-riddled ghost.

T hat history begins in England, in the thirteenth century, when maintaining king's peace became the duty of an officer of the court called a constable, aided by his watchmen: every male adult could be called on to take a turn walking a ward at night and, if trouble came, to raise a hue and cry. This practice lasted for centuries. (A version endures: George Zimmerman, when he shot and killed Trayvon Martin, in 2012, was serving on his neighborhood watch.) The watch didn't work especially well in England—"The average constable is an ignoramus who knows little or nothing of the law," Blackstone wrote—and it didn't work especially well in England's colonies. Rich men paid poor men to take their turns on the watch, which meant that most watchmen were either very elderly or very poor, and very exhausted from working all day. Boston established a watch in 1631. New York tried paying watchmen in 1658. In Philadelphia, in 1705, the governor expressed the view that the militia could make the city safer than the watch, but militias weren't supposed to police the king's subjects; they were supposed to serve the common defense—waging wars against the French, fighting Native peoples who were trying to hold on to their lands, or suppressing slave rebellions.

The government of slavery was not a rule of law. It was a rule of police. In 1661, the English colony of Barbados passed its first slave law; revised in 1688, it decreed that "Negroes and other Slaves" were "wholly unqualified to be governed by the Laws . . . of our Nations," and devised, instead, a special set of rules "for the good Regulating and Ordering of them." Virginia adopted similar measures, known as slave codes, in 1680:

It shall not be lawfull for any negroe or other slave to carry or arme himselfe with any club, staffe, gunn, sword or any other weapon of defence or offence, nor to goe or depart from of his masters ground without a certificate from his master, mistris or overseer, and such permission not to be granted but upon perticuler and necessary occasions; and every negroe or slave soe offending not haveing a certificate as aforesaid shalbe sent to the next constable, who is hereby enjoyned and required to give the said negroe twenty lashes on his bare back well layd on, and soe sent home to his said master, mistris or overseer . . . that if any negroe or other slave shall absent himself from his masters service and lye hid and lurking in obscure places, comitting injuries to the inhabitants, and shall resist any person or persons that shalby any lawfull authority be imployed to apprehend and take the said negroe, that then in case of such resistance, it shalbe lawfull for such person or persons to kill the said negroe or slave soe lying out and resisting.

In eighteenth-century New York, a person held as a slave could not gather in a group of more than three; could not ride a horse; could not hold a funeral at night; could not be out an hour after sunset without a lantern; and could not sell "Indian corn, peaches, or any other fruit" in any street or market in the city. Stop and frisk, stop and whip, shoot to kill.

Then there were the slave patrols. Armed Spanish bands called *hermandades* had hunted runaways in Cuba beginning in the fifteen-thirties, a practice that was adopted by the English in Barbados a century later. It had a lot in common with England's posse comitatus, a band of stout men that a county sheriff could summon to chase down an escaped criminal. South Carolina, founded by slaveowners from Barbados, authorized its first slave patrol in 1702; Virginia followed in 1726, North Carolina in 1753. Slave patrols married the watch to the militia: serving on patrol was required of all able-bodied men (often, the patrol was mustered from the militia), and patrollers used the hue and cry to call for anyone within hearing distance to join the chase. Neither the watch nor the militia nor the patrols were "police," who were French, and considered despotic. In North America, the French city of New Orleans was distinctive in having *la police:* armed City Guards, who wore military-style uniforms and received wages, an urban slave patrol.

In 1779, Thomas Jefferson created a chair in "law and police" at the College of William & Mary. The meaning of the word began to change. In 1789, Jeremy Bentham, noting that "police" had recently entered the English language, in something like its modern sense, made this distinction: police keep the peace; justice punishes disorder. ("No justice, no peace!" Black Lives Matter protesters cry in the streets.) Then, in 1797, a London magistrate named Patrick Colquhoun published "A Treatise on the Police of the Metropolis." He, too, distinguished peace kept in the streets from justice administered by the courts: police were responsible for the regulation and correction of behavior and "the PREVENTION and DETECTION OF CRIMES."

It is often said that Britain created the police, and the United States copied it. One could argue that the reverse is true. Colquhoun spent his teens and early twenties in Colonial Virginia, had served as an agent for British cotton manufacturers, and owned shares in sugar plantations in Jamaica. He knew all about slave codes and slave patrols. But nothing came of Colquhoun's ideas about policing until 1829, when Home Secretary Robert Peel—in the wake of a great deal of labor unrest, and after years of suppressing Catholic rebellions in Ireland, in his capacity as Irish Secretary—persuaded Parliament to establish the Metropolitan Police, a force of some three thousand men, headed by two civilian justices (later called "commissioners"), and organized like an army, with each superintendent overseeing four inspectors, sixteen sergeants, and a hundred and sixty-five constables, who wore coats and pants of blue with black top hats, each assigned a numbered badge and a baton. Londoners came to call these men "bobbies," for Bobby Peel.

It is also often said that modern American urban policing began in 1838, when the Massachusetts legislature authorized the hiring of police officers in Boston. This, too, ignores the role of slavery in the history of the police. In 1829, a Black abolitionist in Boston named David Walker published "An Appeal to the Coloured Citizens of the World," calling for violent rebellion: "One good black man can put to death six white men." Walker was found dead within the year, and Boston thereafter had a series of mob attacks against abolitionists, including an attempt to lynch William Lloyd Garrison, the publisher of *The Liberator,* in 1835. Walker's words terrified Southern slaveowners. The governor of North Carolina wrote to his state's senators, "I beg you will lay this matter before the police of your town and invite their prompt attention to the necessity of arresting the circulation of the book." By "police," he meant slave patrols: in response to Walker's "Appeal," North Carolina formed a statewide "patrol committee."

New York established a police department in 1844; New Orleans and Cincinnati followed in 1852, then, later in the eighteen-fifties, Philadelphia, Chicago, and Baltimore. Population growth, the widening inequality brought about by the Industrial Revolution, and the rise in such crimes as prostitution and burglary all contributed to the emergence of urban policing. So did immigration, especially from Ireland and Germany, and the hostility to immigration: a new party, the Know-Nothings, sought to prevent immigrants from voting, holding office, and becoming citizens. In 1854, Boston disbanded its ancient watch and formally established a police department; that year, Know-Nothings swept the city's elections.

American police differed from their English counterparts: in the U.S., police commissioners, as political appointees, fell under local control, with limited supervision; and law enforcement was decentralized, resulting in a jurisdictional thicket. In 1857, in the Great Police Riot, the New York Municipal Police, run by the mayor's office, fought on the steps of city hall with the New York Metropolitan Police, run by the state. The Metropolitans were known as the New York Mets. That year, an amateur baseball team of the same name was founded.

Also, unlike their British counterparts, American police carried guns, initially their own. In the eighteen-sixties, the Colt Firearms Company began manufacturing a compact revolver called a Pocket Police Model, long before the New York Metropolitan Police began issuing service weapons. American police carried guns because Americans carried guns, including Americans who lived in parts of the country where they hunted for food and defended their livestock from wild animals, Americans who lived in parts of the country that had no police, and Americans who lived in parts of North America that were not in the United States. Outside big cities, law-enforcement officers were scarce. In territories that weren't yet states, there were U.S. marshals and their deputies, officers of the federal courts who could act as de-facto police, but only to enforce federal laws. If a territory became a state, its counties would elect sheriffs. Meanwhile, Americans became vigilantes, especially likely to kill indigenous peoples, and to lynch people of color. Between 1840 and the nineteen-twenties, mobs, vigilantes, and law officers, including the Texas Rangers, lynched some five hundred Mexicans and Mexican-Americans and killed thousands more, not only in Texas but also in territories that became the states of California, Arizona, Nevada, Utah, Colorado, and New Mexico. A San Francisco vigilance committee established in 1851 arrested, tried, and hanged people; it boasted a membership in the thousands. An L.A. vigilance committee targeted and lynched Chinese immigrants.

The U.S. Army operated as a police force, too. After the Civil War, the militia was organized into seven new departments of permanent standing armies: the Department of Dakota, the Department of the Platte, the Department of the Missouri, the Department of Texas, the Department of Arizona, the Department of California, and the Department of the Columbian. In the eighteen-seventies and eighties, the U.S. Army engaged in more than a thousand combat operations against Native peoples. In 1890, at Wounded Knee, South Dakota, following an attempt to disarm a Lakota settlement, a regiment of cavalrymen massacred hundreds of Lakota men, women, and children. Nearly a century later, in 1973, F.B.I. agents, SWAT teams, and federal troops and state marshals laid siege to Wounded Knee during a protest over police brutality and the failure to properly punish the torture and murder of an Oglala Sioux man named Raymond Yellow Thunder. They fired more than half a million rounds of ammunition and arrested more than a thousand people. Today, according to the C.D.C., Native Americans are more likely to be killed by the police than any other racial or ethnic group.

M odern American policing began in 1909, when August Vollmer became the chief of the police department in Berkeley, California. Vollmer refashioned American police into an American military. He'd served with the Eighth Army Corps in the Philippines in 1898. "For years, ever since Spanish-American War days, I've studied military tactics and used them to good effect in rounding up crooks," he later explained. "After all we're conducting a war, a war against the enemies of society." Who were those enemies? Mobsters, bootleggers, socialist agitators, strikers, union organizers, immigrants, and Black people.

To domestic policing, Vollmer and his peers adapted the kinds of tactics and weapons that had been deployed against Native Americans in the West and against colonized peoples in other parts of the world, including Cuba, Puerto Rico, and the Philippines, as the sociologist Julian Go has demonstrated. Vollmer instituted a training model imitated all over the country, by police departments that were often led and staffed by other veterans of the United States wars of conquest and occupation. A "police captain or lieutenant should occupy exactly the same position in the public mind as that of a captain or lieutenant in the United States army," Detroit's commissioner of police said. (Today's police officers are disproportionately veterans of U.S. wars in Iraq and Afghanistan, many suffering from post-traumatic stress. The Marshall Project, analyzing data from the Albuquerque police, found that officers who are veterans are more likely than their non-veteran counterparts to be involved in fatal shootings. In general, they are more likely to use force, and more likely to fire their guns.)

Vollmer-era police enforced a new kind of slave code: Jim Crow laws, which had been passed in the South beginning in the late eighteen-seventies and upheld by the Supreme Court in 1896. William G. Austin became Savannah's chief of police in 1907. Earlier, he had earned a Medal of Honor for his service in the U.S. Cavalry at Wounded Knee; he had also fought in the Spanish-American War. By 1916, African-American churches in the city were complaining to Savannah newspapers about the "whole scale arrests of negroes because they are negroes—arrests that would not be made if they were white under similar circumstances." African-Americans also confronted Jim Crow policing in the Northern cities to which they increasingly fled. James Robinson, Philadelphia's chief of police beginning in 1912, had served in the Infantry during the Spanish-American War and the Philippine-American War. He based his force's training on manuals used by the U.S. Army at Leavenworth. Go reports that, in 1911, about eleven per cent of people arrested were African-American; under Robinson, that number rose to 14.6 per cent in 1917. By the nineteen-twenties, a quarter of those arrested were African-Americans, who, at the time, represented just 7.4 per cent of the population.

Progressive Era, Vollmer-style policing criminalized Blackness, as the historian Khalil Gibran Muhammad argued in his 2010 book, "The Condemnation of Blackness: Race, Crime, and the Making of Modern Urban America." Police patrolled Black neighborhoods and arrested Black people disproportionately; prosecutors indicted Black people disproportionately; juries found Black people guilty disproportionately; judges gave Black people disproportionately long sentences; and, then, after all this, social scientists, observing the number of Black people in jail, decided that, as a matter of biology, Black people were disproportionately inclined to criminality.

More recently, between the New Jim Crow and the criminalization of immigration and the imprisonment of immigrants in detention centers, this reality has only grown worse. "By population, by per capita incarceration rates, and by expenditures, the United States exceeds all other nations in how many of its citizens, asylum seekers, and undocumented immigrants are under some form of criminal justice supervision," Muhammad writes in a new preface to his book. "The number of African American and Latinx people in American jails and prisons today exceeds the entire populations of some African, Eastern European, and Caribbean countries."

Policing grew harsher in the Progressive Era, and, with the emergence of state-police forces, the number of police grew, too. With the rise of the automobile, some, like California's, began as "highway patrols." Others, including the state police in Nevada, Colorado, and Oregon, began as the private paramilitaries of industrialists which employed the newest American immigrants: Hungarians, Italians, and Jews. Industrialists in Pennsylvania established the Iron and Coal Police to end strikes and bust unions, including the United Mine Workers; in 1905, three years after an anthracite-coal strike, the Pennsylvania State Police started operations. "One State Policeman should be able to handle one hundred foreigners," its new chief said.

The U.S. Border Patrol began in 1924, the year that Congress restricted immigration from southern Europe. At the insistence of Southern and Western agriculturalists, Congress exempted Mexicans from its new immigration quotas in order to allow migrant workers to enter the United States. The Border Patrol began as a relatively small outfit responsible for enforcing federal immigration law, and stopping smugglers, at all of the nation's borders. In the middle decades of the twentieth century, it grew to a national quasi-military focussed on policing the southern border in campaigns of mass arrest and forced deportation of Mexican immigrants, aided by local police like the notoriously brutal L.A.P.D., as the historian Kelly Lytle Hernández has chronicled. What became the Chicano movement began in Southern California, with Mexican immigrants' protests of the L.A.P.D. during the first half of the twentieth century, even as a growing film industry cranked out features about Klansmen hunting Black people, cowboys killing Indians, and police chasing Mexicans. More recently, you can find an updated version of this story in L.A. Noire, a video game set in 1947 and played from the perspective of a well-armed L.A.P.D. officer, who, driving along Sunset Boulevard, passes the crumbling, abandoned sets from D. W. Griffith's 1916 film "Intolerance," imagined relics of an unforgiving age.

Two kinds of police appeared on mid-century American television. The good guys solved crime on prime-time police procedurals like "Dragnet," starting in 1951, and "Adam-12," beginning in 1968 (both featured the L.A.P.D.). The bad guys shocked America's conscience on the nightly news: Arkansas state troopers barring Black students from entering Little Rock Central High School, in 1957; Birmingham police clubbing and arresting some seven hundred Black children protesting segregation, in 1963; and Alabama state troopers beating voting-rights marchers at Selma, in 1965. These two faces of policing help explain how, in the nineteen-sixties, the more people protested police brutality, the more money governments gave to police departments.

In 1965, President Lyndon Johnson declared a "war on crime," and asked Congress to pass the Law Enforcement Assistance Act, under which the federal government would supply local police with military-grade weapons, weapons that were being used in the war in Vietnam. During riots in Watts that summer, law enforcement killed thirty-one people and arrested more than four thousand; fighting the protesters, the head of the L.A.P.D. said, was "very much like fighting the Viet Cong." Preparing for a Senate vote just days after the uprising ended, the chair of the Senate Judiciary Committee said, "For some time, it has been my feeling that the task of law enforcement agencies is really not much different from military forces; namely, to deter crime before it occurs, just as our military objective is deterrence of aggression."

As Elizabeth Hinton reported in "From the War on Poverty to the War on Crime: The Making of Mass Incarceration in America," the "frontline soldiers" in Johnson's war on crime—Vollmer-era policing all over again—spent a disproportionate amount of time patrolling Black neighborhoods and arresting Black people. Policymakers concluded from those differential arrest rates that Black people were prone to criminality, with the result that police spent even more of their time patrolling Black neighborhoods, which led to a still higher arrest rate. "If we wish to rid this country of crime, if we wish to stop hacking at its branches only, we must cut its roots and drain its swampy breeding ground, the slum," Johnson told an audience of police policymakers in 1966. The next year, riots broke out in Newark and Detroit. "We ain't rioting agains' all you whites," one Newark man told a reporter not long before being shot dead by police. "We're riotin' agains' police brutality." In Detroit, police arrested more than seven thousand people.

Johnson's Great Society essentially ended when he asked Congress to pass the Omnibus Crime Control and Safe Streets Act, which had the effect of diverting money from social programs to policing. This magazine called it "a piece of demagoguery devised out of malevolence and enacted in hysteria." James Baldwin attributed its "irresponsible ferocity" to "some pale, compelling nightmare—an overwhelming collection of private nightmares." The truth was darker, as the sociologist Stuart Schrader chronicled in his 2019 book, "Badges Without Borders: How Global Counterinsurgency Transformed American Policing." During the Cold War, the Office of Public Safety at the U.S.A.I.D. provided assistance to the police in at least fifty-two countries, and training to officers from nearly eighty, for the purpose of counter-insurgency—the suppression of an anticipated revolution, that collection of private nightmares; as the O.P.S. reported, it contributed "the international dimension to the Administration's War on Crime." Counter-insurgency boomeranged, and came back to the United States, as policing.

In 1968, Johnson's new crime bill established the Law Enforcement Assistance Administration, within the Department of Justice, which, in the next decade and a half, disbursed federal funds to more than eighty thousand crime-control projects. Even funds intended for social projects—youth employment, for instance, along with other health, education, housing, and welfare programs— were distributed to police operations. With Richard Nixon, any elements of the Great Society that had survived the disastrous end of Johnson's Presidency were drastically cut, with an increased emphasis on policing, and prison-building. More Americans went to prison between 1965 and 1982 than between 1865 and 1964, Hinton reports. Under Ronald Reagan, still more social services were closed, or starved of funding until they died: mental hospitals, health centers, jobs programs, early-childhood education. By 2016, eighteen states were spending more on prisons than on colleges and universities. Activists who today call for defunding the police argue that, for decades, Americans have been defunding not only social services but, in many states, public education itself. The more frayed the social fabric, the more police have been deployed to trim the dangling threads.

The blueprint for law enforcement from Nixon to Reagan came from the Harvard political scientist James Q. Wilson between 1968, in his book "Varieties of Police Behavior," and 1982, in an essay in *The Atlantic* titled "Broken Windows." On the one hand, Wilson believed that the police should shift from enforcing the law to maintaining order, by patrolling on foot, and doing what came to be called "community policing." (Some of his recommendations were ignored: Wilson called for other professionals to handle what he termed the "service functions" of the police—"first aid, rescuing cats, helping ladies, and the like"—which is a reform people are asking for today.) On the other hand, Wilson called for police to arrest people for petty crimes, on the theory that they contributed to more serious crimes. Wilson's work informed programs like Detroit's STRESS (Stop the Robberies, Enjoy Safe Streets), begun in 1971, in which Detroit police patrolled the city undercover, in disguises that included everything from a taxi-driver to a "radical college professor," and killed so many young Black men that an organization of Black police officers demanded that the unit be disbanded. The campaign to end STRESS arguably marked the very beginnings of police abolitionism. STRESS defended its methods. "We just don't walk up and shoot somebody," one commander said. "We ask him to stop. If he doesn't, we shoot."

For decades, the war on crime was bipartisan, and had substantial support from the Congressional Black Caucus. "Crime is a national-defense problem," Joe Biden said in the Senate, in 1982. "You're in as much jeopardy in the streets as you are from a Soviet missile." Biden and other Democrats in the Senate introduced legislation that resulted in the Comprehensive Crime Control Act of 1984. A decade later, as chairman of the Senate Judiciary Committee, Biden helped draft the Violent Crime Control and Law Enforcement Act, whose provisions included mandatory sentencing. In May, 1991, two months after the Rodney King beating, Biden introduced the Police Officers' Bill of Rights, which provided protections for police under investigation. The N.R.A. first endorsed a Presidential candidate, Reagan, in 1980; the Fraternal Order of Police, the nation's largest police union, first endorsed a Presidential candidate, George H. W. Bush, in 1988. In 1996, it endorsed Bill Clinton.

Partly because of Biden's record of championing law enforcement, the National Association of Police Organizations endorsed the Obama-Biden ticket in 2008 and 2012. In 2014, after police in Ferguson, Missouri, shot Michael Brown, the Obama Administration established a task force on policing in the twenty-first century. Its report argued that police had become warriors when what they really should be is guardians. Most of its recommendations were never implemented.

In 2016, the Fraternal Order of Police endorsed Donald Trump, saying that "our members believe he will make America safe again." Police unions are lining up behind Trump again this year. "We will never abolish our police or our great Second Amendment," Trump said at Mt. Rushmore, on the occasion of the Fourth of July. "We will not be intimidated by bad, evil people."

Trump is not the king; the law is king. The police are not the king's men; they are public servants. And, no matter how desperately Trump would like to make it so, policing really isn't a partisan issue. Out of the stillness of the shutdown, the voices of protest have roared like summer thunder. An overwhelming majority of Americans, of both parties, support major reforms in American policing. And a whole lot of police, defying their unions, also support those reforms.

Those changes won't address plenty of bigger crises, not least because the problem of policing can't be solved without addressing the problem of guns. But this much is clear: the polis has changed, and the police will have to change, too. ◆

An earlier version of this piece misrepresented the number of Americans between the ages of fifteen and thirty-four who were treated as a result of police-inflicted injuries in emergency rooms.

Race, Policing, and Black Lives Matter Protests

- The death of George Floyd, in context.
- The civil-rights lawyer Bryan Stevenson examines the frustration and despair behind the protests.
- Who, David Remnick asks, is the true agitator behind the racial unrest?

- A sociologist examines the so-called pillars of whiteness that prevent white Americans from confronting racism.
- The Black Lives Matter co-founder Opal Tometi on what it would mean to defund police departments, and what comes next.
- The quest to transform the United States cannot be limited to challenging its brutal police.

Published in the print edition of the July 20, 2020, issue, with the headline "The Long Blue Line."

Jill Lepore, a staff writer at The New Yorker, is a professor of history at Harvard. Her books include "These Truths: A History of the United States" and "If Then: How the Simulmatics Corporation Invented the Future."

P.S. In Conclusion. "TRUMPISM Republicans," are boldly advocating and so blatantly arrogant that since Black man <u>slavery</u>, they now want to **erase** us Nubian and Brown peoples from the America Nubians built, it seems by any means necessary. Almost like Putin's Russia is trying to **erase** Ukrainians off the world's map! Is a fact, and an example is their new "<u>Abortion Laws</u>" which will kill mostly Black women! Vote to say no to their **KKK** police <u>killing</u> innocent unarmed Nubians and other <u>sick</u>, <u>racist</u> **White** **supremacy** <u>hoax</u> practices and leave good, decent, regular hard-working people alone; whether their skin-color is Black, Brown, Yellow, Red or White are all **"God's children"** in **His** sight.

Abu Simbel – The "greatest colossal statured" magnificent **temple,** astonishingly carved in a mountain is the "first in the world" has ever seen, is the cover of this "great little book" it seems America's Mount Rushmore imitated, located in **Nubian** peoples "Sub-Saharan Sudan," **Nubia, Africa.** Lower Nubia on the west bank of upper Lake Nasser and across the River Nile from Qasr Ibrim, about 230 km (140 mi) southwest of Aswan and about 190 miles by road, is in Africa just below that borders Egypt.

The **Nubian** monuments are actually two massive carved rock temples out the mountainside in the 13th century BC, during the 19th Dynasty reign of the Pharaoh Ramesses II. The largest is dedicated to the god Amun, as well as to the Pharaoh Ramesses II himself who ordered the creation of the temple. The second, smaller temple is dedicated to the goddess Hathor and Ramesses II's Queen, is his wife Nefertari and children can be seen in smaller figures by his feet.

During the Egyptian Middle Kingdom years of 2040-1640 BC, the Kingdom of Egypt began expanding in **Nubia**. Egyptians gained control over Nubian trade routes and established "fortresses" down the Nile River. There wasn't much interaction (friction) between the two cultures at this time and it was believed to be fairly peaceful. Nubians were known as "fierce warriors" under Egyptian rule, in archery. They were referred to as the **Medjay,** which originally was an area of land where Nubian's lived and then became to mean an "elite" paramilitary force in the Egyptian army.

While Nubians were "Known" for their "Ferocity" in battle, they still worked in all aspects of ancient Egyptian society including as attendants, merchants, temple employees and also menial jobs. Nubians are believed to be one of the oldest ethnic groups along with their oldest neighbor **Ethiopia,** Nubians having a "rich history and culture."

Nubians originate from the 'central Nile valley area,' many Black historian scholars believe to be **Africa's,** "cradle of civilization" and not the many White historian scholars 'Mesopotamia' Middle-East. They played a large role in ancient Egypt and then, during the medieval period, converted to Christianity and formed three kingdoms was **Nobatia, Makuria,** and **Alodia.** Today, the Nubian people practice Islam, and can still be found in the same area from where they originated from in **Sub-Saharan Sudan.** Nubians can be found living in Egypt, Sudan, and even in **Kenya,** which is famous with Nubian historical sites and African Safari as well.

Even though Nubians reside in two different countries, it is important to remember that they retain their own culture, including their own "5" dialect in languages are: **Nobiin, Kenzi, Midob, Birgid,** and **Kordofan** Nubian. Because of their different languages, Egypt employed Nubian speakers as **"code-talkers"** in the Yom Kipper War against **Israel.** Nubians played an important role in the "rise and success" of ancient Egypt and still are an integral part of the country and today's Egyptian tourism.

The **Temple of Beit-Wali-Beital,** is another temple that was built by Ramesses II. Like Abu Simbel, this was one of Ramesses II Nubian temples built in order to try to maintain Egyptian control over Nubia. The first temple to serve this purpose it's believed.

Temple of Dakka – Originally just a small shrine, the temple of Dakka was expanded during the Roman period and was used as a fortress along the Nile River.

Temple of Maharragua – The temple of Maharragua is a small unfinished temple with an unknown history.

Temple of Amada – The temple of Amada is the oldest temple in Nubia. It was built in the 18th dynasty by pharaoh Thutmose III, and dedicated to Amun and Re-Horakhty. Several pharaohs added to this temple over time included Ramesses II.

Temple of Philae – The temple of Philae is in fact, several temples. This site was known as a place where the goddess **Isis** was worshipped. It also was a popular pilgrimage for Nubians, Egyptians, and travelers from as far as **Greece** and **Crete**.

Temple of Kalabsha – The temple of Kalabsha is relatively new in comparison to other Egyptian temples. It was built around 30 BC during the Roman era. The temple was a tribute to the Nubian sun god **Mandulis,** however, it was never completed.

Temple of Derr – The temple of Derr was also constructed by Ramesses II. It's a "rock-cut temple" and was dedicated to Re-Horakhty.

Temple of Wadi as-Subua – Another "rock-cut temple" built by Ramesses II is another of his Nubian temples. Today, it resides in a valley with two New Kingdom temples.

The Qasr Ibrim – Was once a **"fortress"** and a **"major**

city" perched on a cliff above the Nile River. Today, after the construction of the dam, Qasr Ibrim is actually situated on a rocky island in the middle of the Nile River. Unfortunately, it can't be visited by tourists.

During his reign, Ramesses II embarked on an extensive building program throughout Nubia and Egypt, to which Egypt controlled. Nubia was very important to the Egyptians because it was a source of **"gold"** and many other precious trade goods. He therefore built, several grand temples in Nubia in order to impress upon the Nubian people Egypt's might and Egyptiantize Nubia.

While the Nubian did introduce some of their culture into Egypt, for the most part they kept the same governing rules, artistic style, temples and religious traditions. During this period of time the Nubians also revived the tradition of **"Pyramid Building."** The Nubians ruled over Egypt (**The 25ᵗʰ Dynasty**) **"for a little over 100 years,"** but were eventually pushed out by the **Assyrians.**

After, being overthrown and pushed out of Egypt the Nubians went back to where they originated from and have essentially stayed in the same area throughout time and can still be found in their home there. Many Egyptian Pharaohs, even prior to the 25ᵗʰ Dynasty, had Nubian **blood** running through their veins. Additionally, **"Egyptian Nubians"** tend to be more socio-economically disadvantaged compared to other cultures in Egypt, and often <u>victims</u> of '<u>racism.</u>'

The majority of "Nubian villages" in Egypt today are located near **Aswan** and **Elephantine Island.** These villages are very different than other Egyptian villages and are often easily distinguished from the others by their bright, vibrant colors of green, yellow, red and gold etc. of the houses. Hence, while Nubians who live here are considered to be citizens of Egypt, they still retain their own culture.

An influx of **Arabs** settled in Egypt and the Sudan that means modern day Nubians now follow the **Islamic** faith however, they were convents to Christianity in the "Medieval" period. Nubia, as we know it today, is divided between Sub-Saharan Sudan and Egypt. This happened during the "White man's **colonial** period" and only about a quarter of the Nubian population live in modern Egypt. Again, unfortunately time has not been very kind to Nubians with **<u>racism</u>** that many were forced to leave their **"homes and villages"** Nubians protest which meant nothing up against "progress" along the Nile River, and so the high **"dam of Aswan"** was built.

Construction of the temple complex started in approximately 1264 BC that lasted for about 20 years. It was known as the "Temple of Ramesses, beloved by Amun." However, with the passage of time, all the temples fell into disuse and eventually became almost covered in **sand.** By the 6th century BC, the **"sand"** had already covered the statues of the main temple up to their knees. The temple complex was forgotten until **1813,** when a **Swiss** researcher Johann Ludwig Burckhardt found the top frieze of the main temple.

In **1959,** an international donations campaign started to save the vitally important historic monuments of Nubia. The southernmost relics of this ancient human civilization wouldn't have been under threat, if not for the construction of the Aswan High Dam with rising water of the Nile.

The salvage of the Abu Simbel temples began in **1964** by a multinational team of archeologists, engineers and skilled heavy equipment operators working together under the UNESCO banner; it cost some $40 million US dollars at the time equal to $300 million in 2017 dollars. Between 1964 and 1968, the entire site was carefully cut into large blocks (up to 30 tons, averaging 20 tons), dismantled, lifted and reassembled in a new location 65 meters (195 feet, a 200 feet high building is 20 stories) higher and 200 meters (600 feet, a football field of 100 yards) from the river, in one of the greatest challenges of archaeological engineering in history. Some structures were even from under the waters of Lake Nasser (they say).

Today, a few hundred tourists visit the temples daily. Many visitors also arrive by plane at an airfield that was specially constructed for the temple complex, or by road from Aswan, the nearest city. The complex consists of two temples. The larger one is dedicated to Ra-Horakhty, Ptah and Amun, Egypt's three state deities of the time, and features four large statues of Ramesses II in the façade same appearance. The smaller temple is dedicated to the goddess Hathor, personified by Nefertari the Queen and Ramesses most beloved of his many wives. The temple at present is open to the public.

Nubian people without a doubt, were very intelligent and an integral part of ancient Egypt as we know it. Savvy, clever, but smart about their valuable goods as tradespeople, incredible merciful warriors, and cunning rulers, the great Nubian people played a large role in the creation and success of ancient Black Egypt. As mentioned before, unfortunately in this article time has not been kind to the Nubian people. And to keep White people **scared** of Black people, is the **bigoted,** White **racist** plan. Who seem today in these **last days,** blatantly dare anyone to do something about it, because they can get away with it, they think always… but **Nubians** are the **phenomenal** "wooly haired people" of **"Alfa and Omega,"** "the beginning and the end" under **God…** His "chosen people" in **His image…**

However, as a tourist you can help so much by taking time

to learn more about Nubian culture and pass it on about the "good of a people" and their importance in Egypt, of Nubian Americans, and other Nubians "world-wide." The Nubians of Egypt are a "warm-hearted, kind, and welcoming" people to others, so consider adding a visit to one of their villages into your Egypt tailor made tour.

So ready yourself, to book your trip to Egypt and visit not only the great pyramids but other incredible sites built by Nubians? At **"Osiris Tours,"** we pride ourselves in being one of the best Egypt's luxury tour company, see what you "dreamt" about of histories Nubian **"Abu Simbel."**

Orthodox White man's history is a <u>lie</u> and must be placed back into its proper perspective. A <u>White</u> <u>supremacy</u> <u>veil</u> has thrown us off track somewhat; about world history **"truths"** and who we are as strong Black inventive people they seem to forget, in relationship to everyone else on earth. Whites have many believing they are not only the progenitors (forefather, and originator) of civilization but also the progenitor of **"humanity."** We must first understand in a nutshell Whites are mutated inbred albinos. Since Caucasians cannot reproduce genetic material **"Melanin,"** they could not have spawned (produce or offspring) humanity.

Caucasians birthrates globally are below replacement levels little more than 2%, dwindling also because of their victimization by photolysis. White gene DNA cannot be traced back as far as their genetic parents, BLACK NUBIAN AFRICANS! Because the sun sterilizes and is sending Whites on a course toward extinction, they will not survive independently for very long without people of color depositing their genetic (melanin) material to make their cell replication and reproduction more feasible.

Just about everything we have been led to believe is a myth. White people like to think and want us to believe that they have invented everything that we take for granted in this age. However the truth is, Caucasians have only "REDISCOVERED" the many inventions of OUR BLACK NUBIAN ancestors did **"deep"** in antiquity (prehistory ancient times). Just as they "REDISCOVED AMERICA," with Indian nations already here! Unifying of northern and southern Egypt and Nubia, is preceded by thousands of years of kings that are not taken into account in ancient and prehistory. Egypt did not have a linear (straight) progressive history where they started off primitive and progressed to their ancient history.

NUBIA was the first, then came Egypt as they both started off ADVANCED. Both are the continuation or satellite colonies of an even older and a most fabulous **"super civilization"** everyone, meaning all top nations on earth heard of and are aware of, that Whites erroneously and weren't even created as yet, try pitifully to claim was theirs. There are many ruins and pieces of proof/evidence of the once existence of ATLANTIS.

Not only ancient Plato's account but the megalithic (large or enormous stones used in prehistory monuments) ruins that the United States government is fully aware of off the coast of Bimini. The Bimini Islands, also called Biminis, are a string of Islands, northwestern Bahamas, and West Indies. Bimini is in the Bahamas, only 50 miles away from Miami. Believed to be the remains of the legendary lost empire of Atlantis; that stretches in the Atlantic Ocean easterly in a direction towards our motherland **Africa.**

In perhaps **10,000 BC,** space flight but certainly atomic weapons, may have been the contributing factor in the destruction of Atlantis; is surely a mind-boggling reality with technology similar to we use today in Africa, India, China, Middle East and other South America countries; however, those ruins and pieces of evidence remains have to be the remains of an empire of an ancient **"Black Nubian Civilization,"** that White historians are scared to introduce…perhaps.

There's a 5,000 year old flying machine image etched in a large stone found by American soldiers in an Afghan. Cave. The photographed image source is: Pinterest. Then, Soviet (Russia) scientists discovered old instruments used in navigating cosmic (universe, outer-space) vehicles in caves in **Turkestan** and the **Gobi Desert** (continent of Asia across Mongolia and northwestern China). There are India's Sanskrit texts (there are **five primary sacred texts** of Hinduism), that have references to gods who fought battles in the sky using **Vimana** or (Vimanas) flying vehicles equipped with weapons as deadly as in current times.

Then there's Africa's greatest library at Alexandria that was destroyed by fire that had it not been, for the stupidity from an enemy invasion, the library's contents may have revealed the technology secret of the Black man's use of **"Levitation."** And possible evidence destroyed in <u>hate</u> as well as knowledge in ashes, like India's ancient Indians Viminas flying machine. However, the ancient Indian text from the Ramayana Empire still exists and gives credence to the fact that the Viminas ancient Indian flying machines are a reality and not a figment of some ones imagination.

How old is the Ramayana era? Well, based on astronomical information such as positions of constellations and time of eclipse available in scriptures, they have concluded that events in the Ramayana took place **"7,000 years ago"** and events in the Mahabharata took place **"5,000 years ago.** The Mahabharata <u>war</u> started on October, 3,139 BC. (**5,139 years ago**). White-skin people first appeared on earth **6,000 years ago,** is reasonable could still remember Nubian flying machines handed-down by tribal leader's word of mouth through the generations, and after a while, just didn't let their white masses and others know. It is important that we remember, the inhabitants of the ancient Rama Empire are the ancestors of the Black Dravidians or "Untouchables" (Dalit's) of India today.

It is written in the profound ancient language of Sanskrit, the text give marvelous accounts of really fantastic deadly <u>wars</u> recorded, of strategy fought here on this planet as well as surprisingly in outer space by these ancient flying machines that utilized mercury vortex propulsion. These Vimanas records are not isolated and can be cross-correlated with similar reports in other ancient (like Africa and other) civilizations.

It was also a carefully guarded secret that many of the **"UFO"** sightings of today are actually the **Viminas** of great antiquity being concealed by the United States and other world governments; or reconstructions of those ancient aircrafts is todays, USAF once top secret **"nuclear"** powered **"Flying Triangle" – TR-3B.** The alleged mercury vortex engine that generates a magnetic vortex which effectively neutralizes the effects of gravity on mass.

And so you don't think this is fantasy fiction, we're putting aside human DNA at this time and we'll DNA this flying machine so to speak. A real machinery genetics of mechanical technology we'll call it. Without further delay, the TR-3B is code name for the **Astra,** which is no make believe. The triangular shaped nuclear powered aero -spacecraft platform was developed Top Secret. At least 3 of the **billion** dollar plus TR-3Bs were flying by "1994." The Aurora is the most classified aerospace development program in in existence. The craft is funded and operationally tasked by the National Reconnaissance Office, the NSA, and the **CIA.**

A circular, plasma filled accelerator ring called the Magnetic Field Disrupter, is far ahead of any imaginable technology. The plasms, **mercury** based, is pressurized at **250,000 atmosphere** at a temperature of 150 degrees Kelvin (a temperature scale, which absolute zero is O-K the equivalent of **-273.15 degrees C**) and accelerated to **50,000 rpm** to create a super-conductive plasma with the resulting **"gravity disruption."**

The MFD generates a magnetic vortex field, which disrupts or neutralizes the effects of gravity on mass within proximity, by **89%.** Do not, misunderstand this is **"not anti-gravity"** that provides a repulsive force, that can be used for propulsion. The mass of the circular accelerator and all mass weight within the accelerator, such as the crew capsule, avionics (electronics designed for use in aerospace vehicles), MFD systems, fuels crew environmental systems, and the heavy nuclear reactor, weights are all reduced by **89%,** and the craft can travel at **Mach 9** (7,000 to 8,000 mph), vertically or horizontally. Sources say the performance is not limited to stresses that the human pilots can endure considering the **89%** reduction in mass; the **"G forces"** are also reduced by **89%!!!**

The TR-3Bs propulsion is provided by **3 multimode thrusters** mounted under each corner, of the triangular platform. The TR-3B is a **sub-Mach 9** vehicle until it reaches altitudes above **120,000 feet,** then God knows how fast it can go! The **3 multimode rocket engines** mounted under each corner of the craft uses hydrogen or methane and oxygen as a propellant.

In a liquid oxygen/hydrogen rocket system, 85% of the propellant mass is oxygen. The nuclear thermal rocket engine uses a hydrogen propellant, augmented with oxygen for additional thrust.

The reactor heats the liquid hydrogen and injects liquid oxygen in the supersonic nozzle, so that the hydrogen burns concurrently in the liquid oxygen afterburner. The multimode propulsion system can ; operate in the atmosphere, with thrust provided by the nuclear reactor, in the upper atmosphere, with hydrogen propulsion, and in orbit, with the combined hydrogen/oxygen propulsion. Remember, the **3 rocket engines** are reportedly built by Rockwell. Many sightings of triangular **UFOs** are not "alien" vehicles but the top secret, **TR-3B.**

Creating the TR-3B, modified to the **"TR-3A,"** added on to confuse further the fact that each of these designators is a different aircraft and not the same aerospace vehicle. A TR-3B is as different from a TR-3A as a banana is from a grape. Some of these vehicles are manned and others are unmanned. And in closing here, we at the *Fortney Encyclical History Ed. Co.* realize this has been for you an unexpected reality learning, and an enjoyed great enlightenment in reading. So stay strong, stay wise, have eyes in the back of your head and **fair-you-well!**

Did You Know This? Africa's great civilizations made an immense contribution to the world, which are still marveled at by people today but those who marvel and many more perhaps do NOT know that "**Africans Are the World's First Seafarers.**" Africans crossed the Atlantic Ocean and reached the American continent, perhaps even North America as early as **500 BC**. In the 14th **century**, the **Syrian** writer al-Umari, wrote about the voyage of the Emperor of Mali who crossed the Atlantic with **2,000 ships** but failed to return.

Africans in east and southeastern Africa also set up great civilizations that established important trading links with the kingdoms and empires of **India** and **China** long before Caucasian

Europeans had learned from the Africans how to navigate the Atlantic Ocean. When Europeans first sailed to Africa in the **15**th **century**, African pilots and **navigators** "shared" with them their knowledge of trans-oceanic travel.

It was **"gold"** from the great empires of West Africa, Ghana, Mali and Songhay, which provided the means for the economic take-off of Europe in the **13**th and **14**th **centuries** and aroused the interest of Europeans in Western Africa. An early historian in the **9**th **century** wrote *"The king of Ghana is a great king. In his territory are mines of gold."* When the famous historian of Muslim Spain, al-Bakri wrote about Ghana in the 11th century, he reports that its king *"rules an enormous kingdom and has great power."* The king was said to have an army of **200,000** men to rule over an extremely wealthy empire (by the way, President Obama withdrew **150,000** American troops from **Iraq**).

In the **14**th **century**, the West African empire of **Mali** was larger than Western Europe and reputed to be one of the "largest," "richest" and "most powerful" states in the **"world!"** When the famous emperor of Mali, **"Mansa Musa"** visited **Cairo**, Egypt in **1324**, it was said that he brought so much gold with him that its price fell so dramatically it did not recover its value until **12 years later**.

The empire of **Songhay** was known, amongst other noted things, for the famous world's first university of Sankore based in and called Timbuctu (Timbuktu or Timbuktoo)." Aristotle was studied at **Sankore**, **"Timbuktu"** with subjects like law, various branches of philosophy, dialectic, grammar, rhetoric and astronomy. In the **16**th **century**, one of its most famous scholars, Ahmed Baba, is said to have written more than **40** major books on subjects such as astronomy, history and theology and he had his own private library that held over **1,500 volumes**.

The Muslim invasion of Europe, and the founding of the state of Cordoba, re-introduced all the learning of the ancient world as well as the various contributions made by Islamic scholars and linked Europe much more closely with North and West Africa. So important was the knowledge found in **Muslim Spain**, that one <u>Christian Monk</u> – Adelard of Bath – disguised himself as a Muslim in order to study at the university at Cordoba. Many historians believe that it was this knowledge of **"Muslims"** and definitely the **"African Moors"** brought to Europe through Spain, which not only created the conditions for the **Renaissance** during the middle-ages but also for the eventual expansion of Europe's beginning after Africa's seafaring voyages overseas to the Americas in the last **14**th and early **15**th **century**.

****

Did You Know This? A stout, stand-fast **"Healing Process Remedy for Racism"******* starts with **"Mending Not Avenging History"** either's-way. A **"Mending Anti-African Holocaust In History Academics"** – is with an **"African American Filming Industry;"** interest in achievement movies by **"African American Historians,"** beginnings shown in grammar, high school, and higher schools of education. This would have almost endless topics of the arts and sciences that eventually could spill over into outside entertainment films of authentic histories "War and Peace".

An African American owned filming industry, would be accomplished almost over-night by all players who are champions of big money-making in **"sports."** Our football, baseball, basketball etc. and with the **"Arts"** champions of music's Hip-Hop, Rock & Roll, musician and **"Acting"** stars all together becoming champion contributors; would become **"heroic"** examples, buying mass **share certificates** in their corporate investment of naming perhaps **"HISTORY INC."** an **African American Movie Industry**.

A beginning of academic historical African awareness, short episodes "identity movies" for grammar, then high school and pre-higher schools in public education.

"Biblical Israel Was the Land of Cush"

During the millennial reign of Nubian wooly-hair Christ, an activist liberator for his people, the people, the poor and children Jesus called in anger, "suffer little children to come unto me, and forbid them not: for such is the kingdom of God." Jesus Christ loved and honored little children. Jesus will receive honor from Cush/Ethiopia: "From beyond the rivers of Cush my worshipers, my scattered people, will bring me offerings" (Zephaniah 3:10).

The **Bible** is a reliable, **eyewitness** history criteria of **origin.** Don't over-play leaving no stone unturned towards an advanced lifestyle driven by need. Nubian Americans DNA have much to rise from and **lead** into the **1,000-year period of peace and righteousness** following the second return; of wooly-hair **Nubian Jesus Christ,** who will **"reign"** over the earth during that time…

THE END…"Begins the **American Nubians** being phenomenal people"

ILLUSTRATIONS

He ain't heavy He's my brother

Africa under full glacial conditions

Egypt Sinai Peninsula

****

Egyptians and the Great White Race Map

The ancient connection of Northeast Africa

The Crucifixion

Moses the Law Giver

****

Our Precious Children

3,000 Years Old Helicopter, Submarine ETC.

The Sacred Black Madonna

Akebu-Lan means "Mother of Mankind" Map

Ancient Map of Continental Africa

****

Nubia Region Today Map

Nubian Meroe Pyramids

Ramesses II Storming the Hittite Fortress of Dapur

The Great Nubian is Before the Egyptians

The Giza plateau 3 predominant Pyramids & Great Sphinx

25th Nubian Dynasty/Kushite Tadja

Nubian Winged Goddess

****

REFERENCES

The Fortney Encyclical History Ed. Co. – The World's True Black History, *"First Edition"* by Albert Fortney Jr. 2015; The African Chronologic History is Bible, *"Second Edition"* by Albert Fortney Jr. 2017; The New School Untold History *"Third Edition"* by Albert Fortney Jr. 2019; A Child's Short History Book *Black History Month African Study"* (In cartoon animal characters) by Albert Fortney Jr. 2014; Gold & High-Tech of The Gods *"Fortney Encyclical High-Tech Science"* by Albert Fortney Jr. 2020.

R.T. P Prittchett, scientist in his book, "Natural History of Man," Egyptians was an African Race"

Anthropologist – Count Constain de Volney (1727-1820

Yakub (Nation of Islam) – Wikipedia, the free encyclopedia, Hon. Elijah Muhammad – (expert statements), Hon. Louis Farrakhan – (excerpt statements)

Anthony T. Brower – "Exploding the Myths Vol. 1 Nile Valley Contributions to Civilization"

The Psychology of Racism defining Black History – "Special thanks goes out to," Denzel Caldwell, Nawal Mustafa, Edwin Smit (excerpts total a page)

"Blacked-Out Through Whitewash" by SuZar (r. Epp) Su Zar.com, with thanks from "The New School Untold History" by Albert Fortney Jr. (the grand historian author)

Lepore, J. (2020, July 13). The Invention of the Police. Newyorker. https://www.newyorker.com/magazine/2020/07/20/the-invention-of-the-police

Wikipedia contributors. (2022, September 25). Abu Simbel. In *Wikipedia, The Free Encyclopedia*. Retrieved 20:55, October 3, 2022, from https://en.wikipedia.org/w/index.php?title=Abu_Simbel&oldid=1112245325

Thanks goes out to: Spread the Love – African Tribes descendants of the Hebrew Nation by Nana Kofi